THE AMERICAN KENNEL CLUB'S
Meet the
Beagle™

The Responsible Dog Owner's Handbook

AKC's Meet the Breeds Series

BOWTIE
P R E S S®

Irvine, California
A Division of BowTie, Inc.

An Official Publication of The America... ...ub

AMERICAN
KENNEL CLUB

Brought to you by The American Kennel Club and The National Beagle Club of America.
Lead Editor: Karen Julian
Art Director: Cindy Kassebaum
Production Manager: Laurie Panaggio
Production Supervisor: Jessica Jaensch
Production Coordinator: Leah Rosalez

Vice President, Chief Content Officer: June Kikuchi
Vice President, Kennel Club Books: Andrew DePrisco
BowTie Press: Jennifer Calvert, Amy Deputato, Karen Julian, Jarelle S. Stein

Photographs by: Blackhawk Productions (Dwight Dyke): 34, 62, 73; Cheryl Ertelt: 65; Faith A. Uridel: 24, 37, 80-81, 87, 106; Fox Hill Photo (Daniel Johnson): 72, 75, 79, 86, 92, 109, 121, (Paulette Johnson): 31, 38, 49, 59, 63, 64, 67, 89, 90-91, 99, 105, 110; Gina Cioli/BowTie Studio: cover inset, back cover, 14, 18, 27, 69, 74, 95, 103, 108, 111, 115; LMEimages (Laurie Meehan-Elmer): cover, 30, 32, 43, 44, 45, 52, 57, 58, 66, 70-71, 76, 77, 78, 83, 88, 93, 94, 96, 97, 98, 102, 120; Mark Raycroft Photography: cover insets, 1, 3, 4, 6-7, 8, 9, 10, 11, 12, 15, 16-17, 19, 20-21, 22, 23, 25, 26, 28-29, 40-41, 42, 46, 50-51, 55, 60-61, 68, 82, 85, 100-101, 117; Mary Bloom: 119; Shutterstock: 35, 36, 39, 47, 54, 84, 124; Sporthorse Photography (Tara Gregg): cover inset, 112-113, 114; Wesley Goldstein: 56

BowTie Press®
Division of BowTie Inc.
3 Burroughs, Irvine, CA 92618

Library of Congress Cataloging-in-Publication Data

The American Kennel Club's meet the beagle : the responsible dog owner's handbook.
     p. cm. -- (AKC's meet the breeds series)
  Includes bibliographical references and index.
  ISBN 978-1-937049-98-0
 1. Beagle (Dog breed) 2. Beagle (Dog breed)--Training--Handbooks, manuals, etc. 3. Dogs--Training--Handbooks, manuals, etc. I. American Kennel Club. II. Title: Meet the beagle.
  SF429.B3A44 2012
  636.753'7--dc23
                                2012025436

Printed and bound in the United States
16 15 14 13 12   1 2 3 4 5 6 7 8 9 10

Meet Your New Dog

Welcome to *Meet the Beagle*. Whether you're a long-time Beagle owner or you've just gotten your first puppy, we wish you a lifetime of happiness and enjoyment with your new pet.

In this book, you'll learn about the history of the breed, receive tips on feeding, grooming, and training, and learn about all the fun you can have with your dog. The American Kennel Club and BowTie Press hope that this book serves as a useful guide on the lifelong journey you'll take with your canine companion.

Owned and cherished by millions across America, Beagles make wonderful companions and also enjoy taking part in a variety of dog sports, including Conformation (dog shows), Obedience, Rally®, and Agility.

Thousands of Beagles have also earned the AKC Canine Good Citizen® certification by demonstrating their good manners at home and in the community. We hope that you and your Beagle will become involved in AKC events, too! Learn how to get involved at www.akc.org/events or find a training club in your area at www.akc.org/events/trainingclubs.cfm.

We encourage you to connect with other Beagle owners on the AKC website (www.akc.org), Facebook (www.facebook.com/americankennelclub), and Twitter (@akcdog lovers). Also visit the website for the National Beagle Club of America (http://clubs.akc.org/NBC), the national parent club for the Beagle, to learn about the breed from reputable exhibitors and breeders.

Enjoy *Meet the Beagle*!

Sincerely,

Dennis B. Sprung
AKC President and CEO

6

40

50

112

Contents

CHAPTER ONE

The Happy-Go-Lucky Beagle

Who doesn't know the Beagle? Thanks to Charles M. Schultz, the Beagle is the most famous dog in the world—or so thinks the lovable Snoopy! Even before the launch of the *Peanuts* comic strip in October 1950, everyone in the Western world recognized the merry little hunting hound with the one-of-a-kind name. The Beagle was, in fact, the country's top breed for most of the 1950s, according to American Kennel

A top choice among dog lovers and hunting enthusiasts since the turn of the century, Beagles are family-friendly, energetic hounds with a nose for adventure.

Club registration statistics, and the first choice of families from coast to coast. Who can resist those soft pleading eyes, those cute droopy ears, and that nonstop wagging tail? All dog people—whether hunters, field-trial enthusiasts, dog show folk, or just dedicated pet lovers—easily fall prey to the Beagle's down-to-earth charm, natural charisma, and joy-filled attitude toward everyone he meets.

ARE YOU CUT OUT FOR THE BEAGLE?

Charisma and cuteness certainly go far, but there's more to a Beagle than his smiling face and waving tail. He requires a special owner, one who has time and energy to share. A happy, easygoing approach to life and a strong desire to have fun qualify you as a likely Beagle person. The Beagle is a pawn-sized hound with a king-sized zest for living, and he doesn't like playing alone. Everything is more fun with a friend—or thirty! If you don't mind this little foxhound looking upon you as a human member of his pack, then perhaps a Beagle is for you.

The Beagle is bred in two different heights: 13 inches and under and 15 inches and under. The breed is separated into two sizes for hunting ability in different types of cover. Both sizes make perfectly wonderful urban or field companions.

As a family dog, the Beagle excels. He's not a one-man dog, but considers the whole family—young and old, and everyone in between—his pack. Teach your children how to handle pets and to respect all animals, and the smaller members of your household will most certainly become "Beagle people," too. Beagles take to children like rabbits to the field!

BEAGLE CHORES

For all his muddy glory, the Beagle is a wash-and-wear kind of hound, and you won't waste countless hours grooming your dog or styling his coat. A once-over with a grooming glove or a natural bristle brush and a quick ear-cleaning is all your Beagle requires. It takes about two-and-a-half minutes per day to groom a Beagle's coat, though you'll have to devote another ten or fifteen minutes to vacuum the shed hair left around the house. Yes, Beagles shed, so if an immaculate house is of paramount importance to you, invest in a good Hoover or a reliable cleaning service—or choose a nonshedding breed!

Luckily, the Beagle's a small dog, so house-cleaning chores are minimal compared to those for a Golden Retriever or a Newfoundland. During the winter, your vacuum will get a break as the Beagle's coat thickens up for the colder months and sheds less. Your mop, however, doesn't get a vacation, as Beagles can get just as muddy on a summer hike as they can on a snowy romp. And the mop will come in handy during the first few house-training months, too.

Did You Know?

A popular hare used in Beagle field trials is the snowshoe hare, so called because of the size of its hind feet, found in forests or shrubby swamps across much of Canada and the northern United States, from Alaska to Maine. Unlike rabbits that burrow into the ground when chased, hares run farther, longer, and straighter, making for better sport for Beagles.

A hunting dog by birth, a Beagle won't hesitate to follow his nose toward excitement. Instill strong obedience training in your Beagle from puppyhood.

Speaking of mud and all that goes with it: don't be afraid to give your Beagle a bath! The easiest way to tidy up a muddy Beagle is with a quick, warm bath. It's likely you won't have to do this too often, but a good bath once a month will keep your Beagle smelling fresh.

A VOICE OF HIS OWN

Beagles prefer owners who have patience and a good sense of humor, especially when it comes to commands. In the Beagle's mind, the silliest command of all is *quiet*. Beagles know they've been blessed with a gift to bark, to bay, to howl, to sing! Would you ask Lady Gaga not to give voice to her music? Of course not!

Your Beagle contends that he was "born this way," and he's absolutely correct. Beagles were bred to bark, signaling the location of prey in a hunt. So when your Beagle is excited, he rightly voices his joy and passion. Even though your Beagle will likely not encounter a fox around your home, there may be a jogger passing his fence, a mail truck slowing down at the corner, or a maple leaf falling from a nearby tree without permission! Sometimes the Beagle's bark is a good thing: you will never be surprised by delivery people or strangers.

A BUNDLE OF ENERGY

If you're a jogger, your Beagle will be dancing every time you reach for your sneakers. Beagles will happily accompany you on your morning jog. Because the Beagle's idea of running is following a scent and chasing rabbits, he won't be impressed by your chosen route, but he'll nonetheless keep stride with you. You must always keep your Beagle on leash or else he'll abandon your course the moment he eyes a passing squirrel or smells a hot dog vendor. While your Beagle is young, avoid strenuous exercise. A swift walk or a moderate jog around the block is fine for a young dog, but wait until he's a year old before you attempt a long-distance run.

Physically fit owners are ideal for the Beagle, as exercise accomplishes two important goals for this hound. It keeps him trim and lean, and at the same time it relieves boredom. A Beagle with gallons of energy to burn will be boisterous and barky. If you live in an apartment or condo (or have close neighbors), then you must commit to a good morning and evening exercise routine with your Beagle. Sticking to a schedule provides your dog with structure. All dogs are creatures of habit and prefer knowing what to expect from day to day. On sunny days, you can enjoy a nice leisurely walk with your Beagle, but be sure you've got the right gear for those rainy days, too. Beagles are all-weather dogs, and they

Beagles are happy to be outside in any weather, but take special care that he is protected in especially harsh climates.

Your Beagle may seem apartment-sized on the outside, but he is a country dog at heart. If you live in the city, keep your Beagle on a strict exercise and training schedule to keep his abundant energy in check.

don't mind walking in the rain, sleet, or snow. Be prepared to get out there with your rain slicker or snow boots, hat, and gloves!

COUNTRY, CITY, OR SUBURBS?

Although the Beagle has been climbing the AKC registration stats nationally—number three in 2011—city folk rarely choose this energetic hound. With the exception of a few cities in the South, the Beagle isn't in the top five breeds of any of the largest forty cities in the United States. With their natural propensity for open fields and country life, Beagles may prove a challenge in an urban setting. Even though the Beagle is ideally sized for apartment living, a city Beagle will take more training to keep that recognizable howl in check, and a Beagle owner must do his or her part to keep this hound mentally active and physically exercised.

Think about your home environment and habits before bringing a Beagle into your life. Do you live in an apartment or condo with little access to the outdoors? Do you work long hours? Are you physically active every day of the week? Consider these questions and ask yourself if a Beagle is right for you—and more importantly, are you right for a Beagle?

If you live in a rural area or in the suburbs with a fenced yard, your Beagle will enjoy romping and playing outside, but keep in mind, he's not a self-starter. On inclement days, you'll be tempted to let him outside by himself to do his business, which is fine and much more convenient than walking in the rain. But remember that there's a difference between backyard visits and necessary daily exercise. Your Beagle needs his personal trainer—you—to get him motivated. Take your Beagle on at least two brisk walks a day. If you can accommodate a second dog in your household, think about providing your Beagle with a playmate. Beagles love company, and another canine in your home will provide you and your Beagle with plenty of companionship and entertainment.

If you have a fenced yard, you must remember that not every fence is Beagle-proof. Even though he may only be 15 inches in height at the shoulder (and maybe twice that when standing on his back legs), a Beagle can jump and climb with the near dexterity of a cat. Although Beagles weren't bred to "go to ground" like a terrier, the sight or smell of a varmint (or friendly neighbor) on the other side of the fence will be more than enough inspiration for him to escape. Beagles are as determined as any terrier, so if going over the fence is a problem, they will simply—and swiftly—dig under it. To prevent a Beagle bust-out, you are well advised to install a 6-foot fence and make sure that it is trenched at least 6 inches

Responsible Pet Ownership

Getting a dog is exciting, but it's also a huge responsibility. That's why it's important to educate yourself on all that is involved in being a good pet owner. As a part of the Canine Good Citizen® test, the AKC has a "Responsible Dog Owner's Pledge," which states:

I will be responsible for my dog's health needs.

☐ I will provide routine veterinary care, including checkups and vaccines.

☐ I will offer adequate nutrition through proper diet and clean water at all times.

☐ I will give daily exercise and regularly bathe and groom.

I will be responsible for my dog's safety.

☐ I will properly control my dog by providing fencing where appropriate, by not letting my dog run loose, and by using a leash in public.

☐ I will ensure that my dog has some form of identification when appropriate (which may include collar tags, tattoos, or microchip identification).

☐ I will provide adequate supervision when my dog and children are together.

I will not allow my dog to infringe on the rights of others.

☐ I will not allow my dog to run loose in the neighborhood.

☐ I will not allow my dog to be a nuisance to others by barking while in the yard, in a hotel room, etc.

☐ I will pick up and properly dispose of my dog's waste in all public areas, such as on the grounds of hotels, on sidewalks, in parks, etc.

☐ I will pick up and properly dispose of my dog's waste in wilderness areas, on hiking trails, on campgrounds, and in off-leash parks.

I will be responsible for my dog's quality of life.

☐ I understand that basic training is beneficial to all dogs.

☐ I will give my dog attention and playtime.

☐ I understand that owning a dog is a commitment in time and caring.

into the ground. No matter how determined, bored, or tempted your Beagle becomes, a solid fence discourages him from trying to escape.

Stay active with your Beagle throughout his life. Keep his mind and body occupied, and he will be healthier and happier as a result.

SIMPLY IRRESISTIBLE

The Beagle has been treasured for generations for his jovial personality and limitless happiness. Though infamous for his vocal nature and escape-artist tendencies, the Beagle is the ideal family dog—a Beagle considers all of his human family members, no matter how young or old, as members of his pack, and he is loyal and loving of his family to the extreme. Beagle owners can't resist the breed's zest for life, boundless energy, and droopy-eyed grin—and once you have a Beagle of your very own, you will agree that it's love at first bark.

At a Glance ...

Since the 1880s, the Beagle has been a popular breed choice for dog lovers across the country. Loyal and loving, a Beagle makes the perfect playmate for a young family, and he will quickly adopt both kids and adults as treasured members of his Beagle pack.

Owning a Beagle is not for the weak of heart! Beagles are bred with boundless energy, and your dog will need plenty of exercise to keep him content. Plan at least two brisk walks a day with your adult Beagle, and don't go easy on him—you'll tire long before your Energizer Beagle.

With the boundless joy of the happy-go-lucky Beagle comes a limitless font of energy. Channel that energy into training. Whether it's field trials, agility, or simple commands, your Beagle will benefit—and so will your household—from a good education.

Beagle
Basics

Romantic retellings of the origin of the breed trace the ancestors of today's Beagle back to Greece in 400 BC and eventually to Britain in AD 200. More detailed documentation of hunting hounds appeared in England around the mid-1700s due to the popularity of fox hunting. The two most popular hare hunters were the North Country Beagle and the Southern Hound, two of the earliest types of hound developed. The Southern Hound was

a slow, ponderous dog, while the North Country Beagle was lithe and quick. It wasn't until the 1830s, when wealthy sportsmen began assembling packs for fox hunting, that the Beagle we recognize today came into being.

HOUND GROUP

The AKC Hound Group consists of twenty-seven breeds. Scenthounds and sighthounds are two different kinds of hounds, distinguished by their hunting styles. The Beagle is a nose-first kind of hound, a scenthound, and his fox- and hare-hunting brethren include the English and American Foxhounds, the Harrier, the Basset Hound, and the Petit Basset Griffon Vendéen. The remaining scenthounds in the Hound Group hunt other quarry, such as the aptly named Otterhound; the Dachshund ("badger dog" in German); and the raccoon's most hated quintet, the Black and Tan Coonhound, the Bluetick Coonhound, the Treeing Walker Coonhound, the Redbone Coonhound, and the Plott, a large-game hunter as well as a coonhound. The king of scenthounds, also bred for large game, is the Bloodhound, prized today for his search-and-rescue and trailing abilities. The Beagle, the Bloodhound, and the Otterhound are believed to be the oldest scenthounds in existence.

All of the scenthounds share many behavioral and physical characteristics. These breeds are celebrated for their determination and endurance on the hunt, their musical (to some ears) voices, and their ability to track a specific animal or person. Large nostrils, superior noses, and sensitive, supple ears make it possible for these dogs to gather and track a scent. Although the scenthounds' heights vary from the short Dachshund to the tall Treeing Walker Coonhound, all of these dogs are built for running with strong-boned limbs, well-arched toes, and fluid, efficient movement.

Join the Club

The parent club of a canine breed is considered the expert on everything related to that breed of dog. It's responsible for safeguarding and promoting a particular dog breed. These national organizations are members of the American Kennel Club and are made up of knowledgeable breeders. Each parent club determines the breed standard, denoting the most desired traits of an ideal specimen of the breed, which the American Kennel Club then officially approves. The standard is used to guide breeding practices and competition judging. The parent club of the Beagle is the National Beagle Club of America, founded in the late 1800s. Learn more about the club and its history at its website, http://clubs.akc.org/NBC.

AMERICAN KENNEL CLUB

Most scenthounds have smooth coats like the Beagle, but some breeds come in smooth-, wire-, and long-haired coats, and one (the Dachshund) in all three. Although we are familiar with a short coat on the Beagle, there once was a rough-coated variety as well, similar in coat to the Petit Basset Griffon Vendéen.

A NOSE IS A NOSE

The activity of "walking your dog" is exercise to humans, but to Beagles, it's a scenting expedition. Nose to the ground and march! Every new square of paving cement yields a thousand unexpected scents. You, of course, smell nothing, but your Beagle is filing away cabinets of information in his brain's hard drive: a Dachshund puppy passed by here forty minutes ago; a rabbit stopped on this spot four nights ago, and some rubber-toed human with a runny nose jogged by this

CROUP

BACK

WITHERS

HIP

HOCK

STIFLE

LOIN

BRISKET

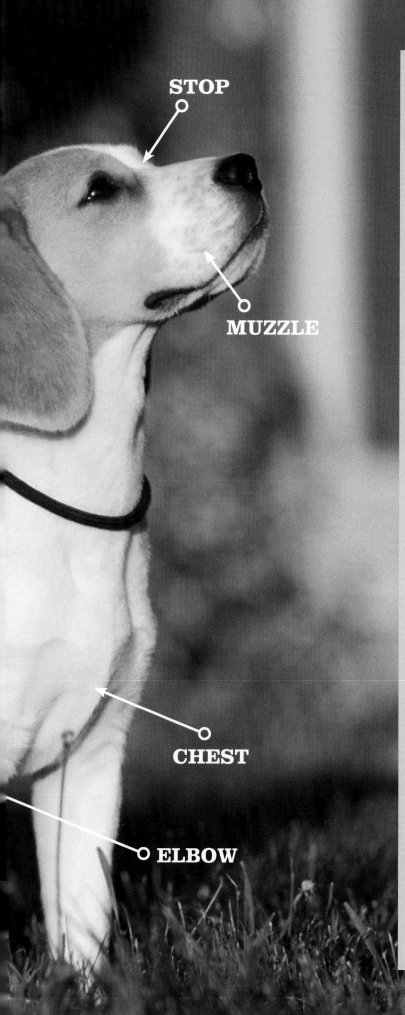

STOP

MUZZLE

CHEST

ELBOW

The Beagle in Brief

COUNTRY OF ORIGIN:
England

ORIGINAL USE:
Rabbit and hare hunting

GROUP:
Hound

AVERAGE LIFE SPAN:
12 to 14 years

COAT:
Close, hard, of medium length

COLORS:
Any true hound color

GROOMING:
Keeping the Beagle neat and clean requires a daily once-over with a hound glove or natural bristle brush. Bathing is required monthly or when the Beagle gets dirty.

HEIGHT/WEIGHT:
The 13-inch variety (up to and including 13 inches) usually weighs under 20 pounds; the 15-inch variety (over 13 inches and under 15 inches) weighs between 20 and 30 pounds.

TRAINABILITY:
Moderate. The Beagle is a classic underachiever who'd rather have a good time than study.

ACTIVITY LEVEL:
High. Beagles need lots of exercise to keep from becoming bored, barky, and destructive.

GOOD WITH OTHER PETS:
Beagles like to be one of a crowd and get along well with other dogs. Beagles aren't reliable around pet rabbits or other small mammals and are prone to give chase.

NATIONAL BREED CLUB:
National Beagle Club of America; http://clubs.akc.org/NBC

RESCUE:
Beagle Rescue Foundation of America; http://brfoa.tripod.com/index.html

Rabbit Farming

Rabbits remain the country's most hunted quarry, and Beaglers recognize that their dogs can only pursue rabbits that are natural inhabitants of the terrain. Rabbits don't acclimate to new grounds as easily as most other types of quarry. The need for a thriving population of wild hares and rabbits led Beaglers to become dedicated conservationists, concerned about the amount of food and natural cover available to rabbits in their terrain. Today, over 500 Beagle clubs own or lease land for field trials and training grounds, most in excess of 150 acres. The clubs' conservationist efforts are often referred to by Beaglers as "rabbit farming."

Meet the Beagle

A great place to see Beagles and more than 200 other dog and cat breeds is at AKC Meet the Breeds®, hosted by the American Kennel Club and presented by Pet Partners, Inc. Not only can you see dogs, cats, puppies, and kittens of all sizes, you can also talk to experts in each of the breeds. Meet the Breeds features demonstration rings to watch events with law enforcement K9s, grooming, agility, and obedience. You also can browse the more than 100 vendor booths for every imaginable product for you and your pet.

It's great fun for the whole family. Meet the Breeds takes place in the fall in New York City. For more information, check out www.meetthebreeds.com.

morning. To a Beagle puppy, the world is fascinating, and his daily walk is second only to mealtime!

It is very difficult for us humans to comprehend the intensity and complexity of the dog's nose, but chew on this for a moment. How often have you smelled an odor that instantly returned you to a moment in your past? The smell of chestnuts roasting transports you to your grandmother's house on Christmas morning when you were ten. Or perhaps, the smell of frying meatballs immediately elicits memories of your mother cooking for you as a child. Scientists refer to these

Your Beagle's nose is an amazing tool that he uses to explore and comprehend the world around him. Let him sniff and smell his fill in the backyard and on walks, but be careful he doesn't follow his nose into mischief.

A PIECE OF HISTORY

There's no definitive answer on how the name "Beagle" came into use. According to the *Oxford English Dictionary*, the Old French word *beegueule*, meaning "open-mouthed," seems to be the most likely origin, referring to the sonorous (big!) voice of this little hunter, whose beginnings are linked to the fox-hounds of France and England.

recollections as odor memories, and it's not a phenomenon unique to humans, other animals experience it as well.

Humans are visually dominant beings, while dogs are nose dominant. The dog's olfactory bulb is estimated to be forty times the size of a human's. The average dog is said to have 125 million smell receptors, scenthounds many more, with Bloodhounds up to 300 million. The dog's nose is believed to be one hundred thousand to a million times stronger than a human's. It's estimated that the best human nose can recognize between four thousand and ten thousand smells, and dogs no less than twenty-five times that number. Imagine the flood of thoughts and ideas entering your Beagle's mind every time he takes a deep sniff. Truly, his whole life (and the lives of others) is passing before his nose!

SNAPSHOT OF THE BEAGLE

The Beagle is a sturdy, compactly built hound, giving the impression of quality without looking coarse. Displaying lots of determination, stamina, and energy, the Beagle is bold, alert, intelligent, and of even temperament.

The AKC standard describes the Beagle's head as having a fairly long skull that is slightly domed at the back, with a broad cranium. The medium-length muzzle is straight and square, with a well-defined stop between the muzzle and face. The jaws are level and the lips free from flews, the pendulous part of the lip that some scenthounds have, such as the Bloodhound.

The Beagle's long, drooping ears are designed to drag against the ground, pushing all scents toward the Beagle's nose.

The Beagle's ears are low-set and long, with rounded tips. The length, size, and shape of the ears assist the Beagle on scent hunts. They are large and long enough to brush against the ground, picking up and retaining the tracked scent.

They should extend nearly to the nose when stretched out and should hang gracefully, close to the cheeks. The eyes of the Beagle are large, with a mild, appealing expression often associated with pleading, gentle hounds.

The throat is free of excess skin, and the strong neck is slightly arched and of sufficient length to allow the hound to reach down easily to scent. The shoulders are muscular, well laid back, and sloping so that the dog can move freely. The Beagle's height from ground to elbow is roughly half the height at the shoulders. The chest is deep and broad, the elbows are firm, and the ribs are well sprung, extending well back, allowing for plenty of lung room.

The Beagle's thighs are muscular for propelling power. When viewed from behind, the legs should be parallel to one another. The feet are tight and firm, well knuckled, and strongly padded. As the Beagle moves, the legs should move with a free stride with drive from the rear. The sturdy tail is set on high and carried gaily, but should not be curled over the back. It should appear short for the size of the dog and is well covered with hair, called "brush," especially on the underside.

The Beagle's coat is short, dense, and weatherproof. It is close and hard. In fact, the AKC standard describes the coat as being of medium length, indicating that it is not short like that of the smooth Dachshund or Miniature Pinscher.

"BIG FOR HIS INCHES"

The AKC standard for the Beagle describes the breed as "a miniature foxhound, solid and big for his inches." For show purposes, the Beagle breed is divided into two varieties: 13 inch and 15 inch. The 13-inch variety is for hounds not exceeding

Each of Beagles features—no matter how cute—are purposeful. The Beagle's square muzzle, long ears, and deep chest are all important for the breed's hunting ability.

The Beagle Breed Standard

General Appearance

A miniature foxhound, solid and big for his inches, with the wear-and-tear look of the hound that can last in the chase and follow his quarry to the death.

Head

The skull should be fairly long, slightly domed at occiput, with cranium broad and full. *Ears*—Ears set on moderately low, long, reaching when drawn out nearly, if not quite, to the end of the nose; fine in texture, fairly broad, with almost entire absence of erectile power-setting close to the head, with the forward edge slightly inturning to the cheek—rounded at tip. *Eyes*—Eyes large, set well apart, soft and houndlike—expression gentle and pleading; of a brown or hazel color. *Muzzle*—Muzzle of medium length—straight and square-cut—the stop moderately defined. *Jaws*—Level. Lips free from flews; nostrils large and open. *Defects*—A very flat skull, narrow across the top; excess of dome, eyes small, sharp and terrierlike, or prominent and protruding; muzzle long, snipy or cut away decidedly below the eyes, or very short. Roman-nosed, or upturned, giving a dish-face expression. Ears short, set on high or with a tendency to rise above the point of origin.

Body

Neck and Throat—Neck rising free and light from the shoulders strong in substance yet not loaded, of medium length. The throat clean and free from folds of skin; a slight wrinkle below the angle of the jaw, however, may be allowable. *Defects*—A thick, short, cloddy neck carried on a line with the top of the shoulders. Throat showing dewlap and folds of skin to a degree termed "throatiness."

Shoulders and Chest

Shoulders sloping—clean, muscular, not heavy or loaded—conveying the idea of freedom of action with activity and strength. Chest deep and broad, but not broad enough to interfere with the free play of the shoulders. *Defects*—Straight, upright shoulders. Chest disproportionately wide or with lack of depth.

Forelegs and Feet

Forelegs—Straight, with plenty of bone in proportion to size of the hound. Pasterns short and straight. *Feet*—Close, round and firm. Pad full and hard.

Hips, Thighs, Hind Legs, and Feet

Hips and thighs strong and well muscled, giving abundance of propelling power. Stifles strong and well let down. Hocks firm, symmetrical and moderately bent. Feet close and firm.

Tail

Set moderately high; carried gaily, but not turned forward over the back; with slight curve; short as compared with size of the hound; with brush.

Coat

A close, hard, hound coat of medium length.

Color

Any true hound color.

Varieties

There shall be two varieties: Thirteen Inch—which shall be for hounds not exceeding 13 inches in height; Fifteen Inch—which shall be for hounds over 13 but not exceeding 15 inches in height. *Disqualification*—any hound measuring more than 15 inches.

—Excerpts from the American Kennel Club Breed Standard

13 inches in height; the 15-inch variety is for hounds over 13 but not exceeding 15 inches in height. Height is measured at the dog's withers (top of the shoulders). This division of the breed into two varieties began in 1893. Newcomers to dog shows often ask why there are two Beagles competing in the Hound Group when most of the other breeds are represented by only one. (Of course, the Dachshund is represented by three.) In 1943, the Best of Variety from both Beagle varieties progressed to the Group competition, so today you will see the winners of the 13- and 15-inch classes competing against each other in the Group.

A HOUND OF ANY COLOR

The breed standard says that "any hound color" is acceptable and that none is more desirable than any other. The classic tricolor pattern in the Beagle is tan, black, and white. The ten most common Beagle colors are: white, black, brown, red, fawn, tan, lemon, blue (a diluted black), bluetick, and redtick. Patterns and markings in the breed include tricolor, bicolor, open, spotted, harepied, merle, and mottled (or ticked). A "merle" pattern is characterized by dark blotches against a lighter background of the same pigment. "Mottled" refers to a pattern of dark roundish blotches superimposed on a lighter background; "ticks" are small spots or freckles.

WHY A BEAGLE?

The joyful Beagle will happily enter your life and your heart. After everything you've learned about the breed's personality and hound-dog good looks, if you still feel that a Beagle is the right choice for your family, take it upon yourself to visit a few Beagle-owning households and breeders. Get to know the Beagle the best way possible—in person! Visit the American Kennel Club website at www.akc.org or the National Beagle Club of America at http://clubs.akc.org/NBC to find Beagle conformation shows or field trials near you. See the Beagle in action! Only then can you make an informed decision on bringing a Beagle—or any dog for that matter—into your life.

At a Glance ...

The Hound Group includes twenty-seven different sighthound and scenthound breeds. The smallest of the scenthound breeds, the Beagle is described as "big for his inches," true on many levels, as the breed's personality and carriage are anything but small. The Beagle's limitless joy and jovial nature will quickly capture the heart of any owner.

. . . .

Any hound color is acceptable in the Beagle, including but not limited to white, black, brown, red, fawn, tan, lemon, blue (a diluted black), bluetick, and redtick.

. . . .

The Beagle is separated into two height varieties: under 13 inches and between 13 and 15 inches. It is the only breed in the Hound Group that is divided into two classes based on height.

CHAPTER THREE

Finding a Beagle

Charlie Brown's black-and-white pet dog isn't the "ideal Beagle" by any means. You'd never waste words like "warm personality" or "no gentler, more trustworthy friend" on Snoopy! And yet, there is a certain charm about this fictional hound, so much so that we can't ever take anything away from this pen-and-ink Beagle of Beagles. He's clearly more clever and resourceful than the rest of the *Peanuts* gang, and, as the Red Baron, he would

Finding a responsible, experienced breeder is as important as choosing the right puppy. Do the research and don't rush the process. Finding a healthy puppy is worth the wait.

certainly "chase and follow his quarry to the death," as concludes the AKC breed standard.

FINDING A BREEDER

Your quest to find your dream Beagle, not a fictional character, but a real, live, wonderful purebred puppy, begins now! Because the breed is very popular in the United States and continues to rank high in AKC registrations—number three in 2011—you'd think that finding a good Beagle breeder would be easy. You may be fortunate enough to live in close proximity to a good breeder, but be prepared to travel to find the right puppy. The time and money spent finding a responsible breeder will be well worth it.

It's best to begin your puppy search online. Visit the AKC's website at www .akc.org to search for a Beagle breeder in your area. The breeder-classifieds page allows you to select the breed of your choice and the number of miles you're willing to drive. Try to find a breeder who is listed as an AKC Breeder of Merit program participant. Ideally, the breeders listed will also be members of the National Beagle Club of America and various other local AKC-licensed clubs.

Your second online visit should be to the National Beagle Club of America's website at http://clubs.akc.org/NBC where you will find a list of NBC members or supporting members who breed puppies. The breeders are listed by state, and most provide phone numbers, websites, and e-mail addresses that you can use to get in touch with them. The NBC site includes mainly breeders who specialize in

Don't fall for the first pair of pleading Beagle eyes you see. Visit at least two or three breeders and their litters before deciding on a puppy.

show pups, though some focus on field and obedience competition as well. The parent club doesn't endorse these breeders or guarantee the health or breeding of their dogs, so new owners are encouraged to do their homework and further research each breeder before purchasing a puppy.

When looking for a breeder, consider the following criteria:

- Membership in the National Beagle Club of America (NBC) and possibly a regional Beagle club (if there's one in the area)
- No fewer than five years showing and breeding Beagles
- Registration of all litters and puppies with the American Kennel Club
- Participation in AKC dog shows, Beagle field trials, and/or obedience trials
- Support of local Beagle rescue efforts
- Champion certificates and trophies to indicate success in AKC competitions
- Participation in the AKC's Breeder of Merit program, signifying that the breeder has been active in the breed for no fewer than five years and has earned at least four titles on dogs he or she has bred or co-bred
- Willingness to answer all questions freely, to accept the puppy back if you are unhappy for any reason, and to guarantee the puppy's health
- References from other puppy owners
- Maintenance of a limited breeding program, producing only one or two litters per year

You can also find a qualified, reputable breeder by visiting a local dog show. There are shows in every region of the country on almost every weekend of the

Did You Know?

In England, where the breed developed, there is only one height clause in the breed standard, with a minimum height of 13 inches (33 cm) and a maximum height of 16 inches (40 cm). Here in the United States, any Beagle measuring more than 15 inches is disqualified from conformation shows as well as field trials.

year, and the AKC website (www.akc.org) provides a complete listing of the shows, times, and locations. Even if you're not looking for a puppy to compete in conformation events, dog shows are ideal places to meet breeders and other people active in purebred dogs. There is no better way to find out if the Beagle breed is for you than to talk to these Beaglers. Real Beagle people will be happy to advise you, provide recommendations, and welcome you into the Beagle pack. Most Beaglers are as gregarious and friendly as the hounds that they so greatly admire.

WHAT TO EXPECT

Fortunately for Beagle lovers, there are many good breeders around if you look carefully. But even with a personal recommendation, you still need to be sure that the breeder's standards of care are what you expect. You must also be certain that the breeder fully understands the breed and has given careful consideration to the way his or her Beagles have been bred, taking pedigree, health screening, and temperament into consideration.

The breeder you select may be someone who raises the puppies in his or her home, in which case they will hopefully have been socializing the pups with

When choosing a puppy, watch how each pup interacts with his littermates. This will give you an idea about his personality, whether he is outgoing, shy, or playful.

all the common household activities and noises that surround them. However, the breeder may run a larger establishment, with Beagle puppies raised in a kennel situation; if you have chosen wisely, the breeder will have socialized the puppies with lots of human contact and exposure to various sounds. Beagles thrive in kennel environments, so you needn't worry if the litter was raised in a kennel. However, if you are planning on raising your Beagle in a family environment, finding a breeder that whelps his or her litters inside the home is preferred. Whether in the home or in a kennel, it is important that the conditions are clean, and the puppies should be well supervised in a comfortable environment.

The breeder should be perfectly willing to show you the dam (mother) of the litter, and it will be interesting for you to take careful note of her personality and temperament and how she interacts with her offspring. If the dam is not available

Be a Smart Shopper

Your local newspaper is not a good resource for buying a puppy. Most reputable breeders have a waiting list and don't need to advertise their litters in the general media. Take your time and don't rush the process. Use common sense: ignore the flyer in the local supermarket as well as any website that doesn't include references or links to the AKC and the NBC. Approach the search with much thought and dedicated research.

Get Your Registration and Pedigree

AMERICAN KENNEL CLUB

A responsible breeder will be able to provide your family with an American Kennel Club registration form and pedigree.

AKC REGISTRATION: When you buy a Beagle from a breeder, ask the breeder for an American Kennel Club Dog Registration Application form. The breeder will fill out most of the application for you. When you fill out your portion of the document and mail it to the AKC, you will receive a Registration Certificate proving that your dog is officially part of the AKC. Besides recording your name and your dog's name in the AKC database, registration helps fund the AKC's good works such as canine health research, search-and-rescue teams, educating the public about responsible dog care, and much more.

CERTIFIED PEDIGREE: A pedigree is an AKC certificate proving that your dog is a purebred. It shows your puppy's family tree, listing the names of his parents and grandparents. If your dog is registered with the AKC, the organization will have a copy of your dog's pedigree on file, which you can order from its website (www.akc.org). Look for any titles that your Beagle's ancestors have won, including Champion (conformation), Companion Dog (obedience), and so forth. A pedigree doesn't guarantee the health or personality of a dog, but it's a starting point for picking out a good Beagle puppy.

for you to see, this might be a sign that the puppy was not born on the premises, but has been brought in from another breeder to be sold.

As for the sire (father), it is likely that he will not be available, for he may be owned by someone else, and a careful breeder may have traveled hundreds of miles to use his stud services. This is completely normal and acceptable for seasoned breeders. Nonetheless, most dedicated breeders will be able to show you a picture of him or at least provide a pedigree for him.

Ask the breeder what health concerns he or she has encountered in his or her line. The breeder should be happy to see that you're researching the breed and taking this acquisition seriously. Though there are no health screening requirements for Beagles, responsible breeders screen the parents of their puppies prior to breeding and should be knowledgeable about any potential problems in their dogs. Breeders who belong to the National Beagle Club of America will be aware of the various screening recommendations for Beagles. In the United States, many breeders register the results of hip tests with the Orthopedic Foundation for Animals (OFA) and eye tests with the Canine Eye Registration Foundation

(CERF). It's important for potential owners to do their best to find Beagles that do not come from unhealthy lines. The money you save on a "bargain puppy" may cost you many times your savings at the vet's office.

COMMON QUESTIONS

You will no doubt have plenty of questions for the breeder. But be prepared for the breeder to ask you questions as well. Responsible breeders want to know that their puppies are going home with trustworthy owners. They have put a lot of time, effort, and money into their litters, and they want to learn as much about you as you do about them. Here are a few questions that your breeder may ask:

1. **What made you choose a Beagle?** Breeders want to know that you have done your research on the breed and know what to expect from a Beagle in personality and behavior. They also want to know about your history with dogs in general. Have you ever owned a dog before? If so, tell your breeder all about it. If not, explain why you want a dog and why you feel that you will make a great Beagle owner.

2. **Do you live in an apartment or in a single-family home?** This is an important question as many apartment associations do not allow dogs. The breeder wants to be sure that you have checked with your association ahead of time and gained permission to own a dog. Don't be surprised if your breeder asks for written approval from your association or landlord. If you live in a

Why Should You Register with the American Kennel Club?

Registering your puppy with the American Kennel Club helps the AKC do many good things for dogs everywhere, such as promote responsible breeding and support the care and health of dogs throughout the country. As a result of your registration, the AKC is able to inspect kennels across the country, educate dog owners about the importance of training through the Canine Good Citizen® Program, support search-and-rescue canines via the AKC Companion Animal Recovery Canine Support and Relief Fund, teach the public about the importance of responsible dog ownership through publications and the annual AKC Responsible Dog Ownership Days, and much more. Not only is the AKC a respected organization dedicated to the registration of purebred dogs, but it is also devoted to the well-being of dogs everywhere. For more information, visit the AKC registration webpage at www.akc.org/reg.

Girl or Boy?

Though both male and female Beagles are very similar physically, they do have a few personality differences that may sway your decision one way or the other. Male Beagles can be more protective of their homes and have the urge to roam—making them more talented and persistent escape-artists than your average female Beagle. Females, however, have the tendency to be moody when in heat. No matter your choice, if you decide to spay or neuter your Beagle, most if not all of these personality differences are minimized significantly, leaving your Beagle—whether male or female—simply a Beagle.

single-family home, do you have a backyard that is securely fenced? Above all, your breeder wants to know that you are going to raise your puppy in a safe and secure environment.

3. What are your normal working hours? If you work full-time, be prepared to explain how you will provide for your Beagle during the long work day. Will you be taking your dog to doggy day care, or will you have a neighbor check in on your dog during the day? Your Beagle will quickly grow bored and become destructive—or worse, try to escape—if he is left alone all day. Think about how you will provide for your Beagle while you are away from home.

4. Do you have any children? Beagles are wonderful family dogs that get along very well with children. That being said, you still need to teach your children how to act and be respectful around a dog. Explain to your breeder how you plan on introducing your children and monitoring their play with the new puppy.

5. How are you planning to train your Beagle? A mischievous Beagle needs more than just basic obedience training. Though you may never have a champion of obedience, you should plan on enrolling your Beagle in a few puppy kindergarten and basic obedience training courses. Talk to your breeder about this and get his or her recommendations. Your breeder knows Beagles and their personalities better than anyone!

SELECTING A PUPPY

When you go to the breeder to visit a litter of puppies, you are certain to be excited, and the puppies will be excited to see you, too. Try not to pick up and cuddle them immediately, but first watch how they play with each other and how they react to you. Bear in mind that Beagles often like to play with their mouths, mouthing and tasting everything in reach; this is not an angry gesture or one of fear, it's simply the way they like to have fun.

Healthy puppies should be clean, without any signs of discharge from eyes or noses. Their bottoms should be spotless, with no indication of loose bowels or diarrhea. Although puppies' nails can be sharp, they should not be overly long. The breeder should clip them as necessary.

Coats should be soft and resilient, with that unmistakable clean puppy smell. Keep your eye out for any parasites, such as lice, mites, or fleas. These tiny bugs cannot always be seen easily, but you might notice a rash or a puppy that is excessively scratching himself. Scratching, though, does not necessarily indicate a parasitic or skin condition, for it is also associated with teething. If the discomfort is due to teething, the puppy will only scratch around his head and muzzle area. This will stop around seven or eight months old when his second set of teeth has fully come in and his gums are no longer sore. On the other paw, scratching might also be connected with an ear infection, so a quick look inside the ears will ensure that there is no odor, redness, or buildup of wax.

Although Beagles can sometimes be a little reserved with strangers, they are social animals by nature and their temperament is generally friendly. Expect a Beagle puppy to be friendly and eager to meet you, and do not take pity on the overly shy one that hides away in a corner. Your chosen puppy should clearly enjoy your company when you arrive to visit. When you go to select your puppy,

Ask the breeder to see the mother and father of the litter. The parents should be friendly, healthy, and outgoing—exactly what you want your puppy to be like as an adult.

take the members of your immediate family with you. It is essential that every member agrees on the important decision you are about to make, for a new puppy will inevitably change all of your lives.

ONCE YOU'VE DECIDED

Most breeders will allow you to visit and select a puppy at about five or six weeks old, but responsible breeders will not let you take the puppy home until he is about eight or ten weeks old. During this crucial time, your breeder will begin socializing your puppy to human contact and all of the common noises around the house, such as the dishwasher, doorbell, vacuum cleaner, and television.

When you do finally choose a puppy, your breeder will put together a large packet of materials for you to read and keep on file for future use. This packet should include a sales contract, pedigree and registration papers, and the puppy's health certifications and vaccination history (as well as the health certifications of his mother and father). Some breeders will also give you a small quantity of food to take home with you, but in any event they should always provide written details of exactly what type and quantity of food is fed, and with what regularity.

The sales contract is essential to the transaction between you and the breeder.

Choose the healthiest puppy you can find. Don't pick a pup simply based on his cost. A "discount" puppy will cost you much more in future veterinary bills and heartache.

The contract should outline the puppy's cost, health guarantees, and return policies if things do not work out. The contract may also include a spay or neuter requirement if you will not be showing your puppy. Do not purchase a puppy without getting all of the breeders' guarantees and promises in writing. You want to be sure that you are legally protected if anything is amiss with your puppy's health and/or pedigree.

The breeder should have already registered the litter with the American Kennel Club upon its birth. The breeder will provide you with a partially filled out AKC Dog Registration Application for you to finish and mail to the AKC or submit online at www.akc.org. With this application, your breeder should also provide you with your puppy's pedigree, detailing your Beagle's ancestry going back at least three generations. This proves that your puppy is descended from a pure-bred Beagle line and is applicable for AKC registration.

Your Beagle puppy should have already been examined by a veterinarian and received some of his first vaccinations by the time you bring him home. Your breeder will provide you with a health certificate that confirms the puppy's good health and details which vaccinations the puppy has received. Details about the puppy's worming routine will also be described in this paperwork. Don't hesitate to ask to see the health certificates of the puppy's parents as well. Take copies of all of this information to your first veterinary appointment so that your vet has a complete medical history for your pup.

The best breeders care deeply about the well-being of their puppies, and they should be more than willing to take back the dog at any time if you can no longer care for him. The breeder should also be a mentor to you throughout your Beagle's life. If you have any questions on feeding, care, or behavior, your breeder will be happy to help you by giving you ample advice and suggestions.

ODDS AND ENDS

Hopefully you will have already done plenty of research about the breed long before you decide to add a Beagle to your life. Books about the Beagle should be available in book stores and pet shops, and as your interest and knowledge in the breed grow, so too should your library. The world of owning Beagles, Beagling, and showing Beagles is ever expansive and makes for fascinating reading.

Finally, it is a good idea to become a member of at least one breed club. There are no fewer than two dozen specialty clubs for Beagles, not to mention a couple of hundred field-trial clubs dedicated to Beagles. You can access a list of these clubs on the AKC website (www.akc.org) or on the National Beagle Club of America website (http://clubs.akc.org/NBC). As a member of one of these local clubs, you will receive notification of breed-club specialty shows, all-breed dog shows, as well as field trials. These various events may be interesting to you and provide new opportunities to learn about the Beagle. Even if you choose not to participate, it's fun and exciting to see your favorite breed, the Beagle, in action.

At a Glance ...

The key to finding the perfect Beagle puppy is to first find a responsible breeder. Use internet resources such as the American Kennel Club website (www.akc.org) and the National Beagle Club of America website (http://clubs.akc.org/NBC) to begin your search, and then ask your veterinarian or trusted Beagle-owning friends for advice and recommendations.

. . . .

Choose a healthy puppy with an upbeat and outgoing personality. It may be tempting to choose the shy runt of the litter, but this may lead to expensive veterinary bills or training classes in your future. It's best to start off on the right foot and choose the happiest and healthiest Beagle puppy you can find.

. . . .

Don't purchase a puppy without a sales contract, pedigree and registration papers, and health certifications not only for your puppy but for his parents as well. These documents will help assure you of your Beagle puppy's health and good breeding.

Your Beagle's New Home

Before inflating the "Welcome Home, Puppy" balloons, there are a few things you must do (and a few items you must buy) to prepare for your puppy's arrival home. It's always best to be a few steps ahead of your new bundle of Beagle joy. Once the puppy's paws cross your front doorstep, you will have a full-time job supervising your Beagle to keep him out of trouble. You'll have less time for chores and errands until your puppy is more trustworthy

In the Dog House

Snoopy's favorite sleeping spot is lying flat atop his little red dog house. That's all the shelter he needed come sun, rain, wind, or snow. In reality, Beagles need much more shelter than just a small dog house. Your Beagle should be kept indoors during the heat of the day and at night. You can provide him with a dog house of his very own, but keep in mind that this will not act as adequate shelter for him throughout the day. Dog houses are prone to get dangerously hot in the midday sun, and your Beagle will get quickly overheated. Garages, patios, and sheds are no exception. The only acceptable place for your Beagle to spend the majority of his day and night is in the house with the rest of the family where the temperature is controlled.

around the house. Caring for a Beagle puppy can be demanding at times—but it is sure to be a lot of fun!

SHOPPING FOR YOUR PUPPY

Before hitting the stores, talk to your breeder about the basic supplies you'll need. Find out what kind of collar and leash he or she prefers to use on Beagle puppies. The breeder may also have a recommendation for which style of crate works best in his or her experience. Take full advantage of the breeder's experience and ask for as much information and as many recommendations as possible.

If you live close to a pet-supply superstore, take a look at their available dog supplies, but be prepared to be a little overwhelmed by the selection that you'll find there. There are multiple aisles of dog food, toys, collars and leashes, beds, crates, and grooming supplies—be sure you have a list of what you're looking for before you enter. A smaller pet shop will have a more limited selection, but it may have the advantage of a more knowledgeable staff who can offer you guidance on your purchases.

Another fun option for dog-supply shopping is a large, all-breed dog show. Not only will you meet crowds of dog-loving enthusiasts but you can also peruse the wares available at the many trade and product stands that cater to the most discriminating fanciers.

THE ESSENTIALS

Aisles and aisles of dog supplies await you at your local pet store, but there are really only a few essentials that you will need for your Beagle puppy during his

first months. Here are a few suggestions of what to look for when shopping for your new puppy:

Grooming supplies: Beagle owners will save money in this department! A slicker brush, a soft-bristle brush, and a hound glove are the only three grooming tools you'll need. Because a bath is inevitably in your pup's future, a good-quality puppy shampoo should be on your list as well. Additionally you should purchase a scissor- or guillotine-style dog-nail trimmer and file. When it comes to grooming supplies, don't look for a bargain. Purchase the best-quality equipment you can find so that you don't have to replace it in the future.

Feeding bowls: The easiest bowls to clean are stainless steel. Lightweight and indestructible, they can be sanitized in the dishwasher. Stainless steel bowls may not be as fun or colorful as ceramic or plastic bowls, but they're the best investment. Ceramic bowls are easily broken by a boisterous Beagle, and plastic bowls can be chewed and harbor bacteria if not cleaned properly. Some dogs can also develop allergies to plastic and acquire mouth sores and acne. How many food and water bowls should you purchase for your Beagle? Buy no fewer than

Purchase only a few toys at first to learn which types your puppy will enjoy most. Start out with a basic rope toy, squeaky toy, and stuffed toy, and see which is the favorite.

three: one for food and two for water (one indoors and one outdoors). Always have fresh, cool water available for your Beagle at all times.

Crate: The crate is the best option for your dog's sleeping accommodations and for house-training. Whether your Beagle pup is going to be a pet, a show dog, or a field dog, the crate is the best place for him to sleep. The crate should be both sturdy and portable. During his first night, when your restless newcomer begins to whine—and yes, he will whine—you can easily carry the crate and place it in the corner of your bedroom. The pup will be able to hear you, see you, and smell you. Whatever you do, leave him in his crate. Don't give in to his pleas and let him sleep in your bed. Your Beagle needs to understand that you are the leader of the house, and he will consider himself your equal if you let him sleep in bed with you.

Crate pad: You can purchase a washable, fleece crate pad to fit perfectly inside the crate. Your Beagle will appreciate the softness and warmth when he's ready for sleeping. During the day, you may want to remove the

The first few weeks with your puppy are important, as he is learning what is expected of him. Be supportive, positive, and consistent, and your puppy will learn the rules of the house in no time.

crate pad and place a couple of towels inside the crate until your Beagle is house-trained. Once he is house-trained, you can purchase more comfortable, permanent bedding for his crate.

Bed: Your puppy will welcome a soft, cushioned dog bed and enjoy curling up on it. Place it in the room where you and your family spend the most time. Purchase a medium-sized bed, which will be a little large for the puppy, but he'll soon grow into it. Select a dog bed that is durable and easily laundered as accidents are inevitable. A removable cover that can be easily unzipped and tossed in the washing machine will save you time and aggravation. Keep your dog's bedding clean and dry at all times, and position the bed so that it's away from drafts and foot traffic.

Gardeners Beware

Fruits and vegetables should be on every healthy Beagle's menu, though not all fruits, vegetables, and plants are good for dogs. If you're a gardener and have a prized lemon grove or even a small patch of heirloom tomatoes, keep your Beagle away. The ASPCA provides a list of approximately four hundred toxic plants that dog owners should keep away from dogs. Visit www.aspca.org for the complete list, including photographs, descriptions, and clinical signs of toxicity of each plant. Here's a brief list of the most recognizable:

- Apple
- Avocado
- Bird of Paradise
- Carnation
- Chrysanthemum
- Coffee
- Daffodil
- Daisy
- Elephant Ears

- Eucalyptus
- Garlic
- Gardenia
- Grapefruit
- Holly
- Hydrangea
- Lemon, lime, and orange
- Lily of the Valley

- Macadamia nut
- Mistletoe
- Oleander
- Onion
- Peach
- Plum
- Poinsettia
- Tomato
- Tulip

Toys: Beagles love to play, as do most dogs. Play is part of a dog's social life, and toys are every puppy's favorite accessories. Don't overwhelm the puppy with a toy box filled with dozens of playthings. Begin by selecting a chew toy (a nylon bone or hard rubber teething ring), a soft, plush object with a squeaker, and a ball or two. Not every toy will have the same appeal to your puppy, and there's no predicting which ones he will like until you try them out. Some dogs go wild for squeaky toys and others aren't very interested. Always keep the safety of your dog in mind when purchasing toys. Routinely check toys for any loose parts that a curious puppy could swallow.

BEAGLE-PROOFING

Small, active dogs such as the Beagle can easily get into mischief around the house, so you must be prepared to minimize the

The Great Escape

Beagles are known for their ability to escape even the most high-security yards. This little hound will follow his nose wherever it leads—out the door, across the grass, over (or under) the fence, and down the street! It's important to secure your yard with at least a 6-foot wooden or cement-block fence (you'd be surprised how well your Beagle can climb chain link), that also burrows into the ground at least 6 inches. And just to be safe, it's important that your Beagle be microchipped and always wear a collar with identification tags.

temptations. Led around the floor by his unstoppable nose, your Beagle will sniff and hunt until he finds something fun to investigate. The best way to Beagle-proof your house is to get down on all fours and explore every room that is open to your dog from his vantage point. It's amazing how different things look from the floor and how quickly dust and clutter accumulates. From this Beagle-perspective, you'll find old candy wrappers, spare coins, and loose wires under beds, behind bookshelves, and in between couch cushions. Remember that your Beagle is a scenthound, and he will inhale lots of dust and dirt as he sniffs about the floor. After you've secured and thoroughly puppy-proofed the room, grab a mop and clean the floor.

Here is a list of some everyday household things that you must cover or remove from the puppy's reach:

- Electrical cables
- Shoes, socks, and other articles of clothing
- Breakable ornaments on low tables
- Household cleaners, polishes, and other solutions
- Fertilizers and yard tools
- Antifreeze, bleach, gasoline
- Candy on the coffee table
- Table cloths, table runners, and pillows with tassels
- Small articles that can be swallowed (paper clips, tacks, etc.)
- Houseplants that can be toxic to pets
- Outdoor garbage cans and indoor trash cans

In addition to puppy-proofing, the best way to keep your puppy out of trouble is to restrict his access to the whole house. When you first bring your puppy home, close bedroom doors and use baby gates or exercise pens (also known as X-pens) to keep your puppy confined to only the rooms you have fully secured. The kitchen and living room are usually good places to start with as this is where you spend most of your time. As your Beagle becomes more confident and trustworthy, slowly give him more access to the house room by room.

If you need to leave your puppy unsupervised for a short time to run errands, to shower, or to do some chores, place your dog in his crate or confine him to a small area that is surrounded by baby gates or an exercise pen. Be sure that this area is on a wood or tile floor that can be cleaned easily when your puppy has an accident. Place your dog's crate, his food and water dishes, and a few toys in the area with him. Also place a piece of newspaper in the area where he can relieve himself. Leave your puppy in this area for short times at first so that he gets used to being alone without becoming frightened. Get into the habit of leaving him alone for an hour or two each day. This will allow him to become comfortable with being alone and will help avoid separation anxiety in the future.

A SOCIAL HOUND

Once your puppy has had a day or two to get comfortable around the house, make a conscious effort to have him experience the many strange household

A PIECE OF HISTORY

In the 1500s, British royals including Queen Elizabeth I fancied the tiniest Beagles, which were called "Glove Beagles" or "Pocket Beagles." These little foxhounds, said to be only 9 inches in height, were carried in the pockets of hunters on horseback or in their pannier bags. While small Beagles exist today, none would fit in your pocket! Avoid breeders who specialize in "Pocket Beagles," as they are usually unscrupulous and counting on uninformed buyers to fall for their gimmick.

sounds that surround him. The idea is to desensitize your Beagle to noises that he might find scary or startling. For example, most dogs perceive the vacuum as a threatening alien and will bark at it or even try to attack it. While your dog is playing with a favorite chew toy, turn the vacuum cleaner on in a nearby room so that he can hear it. In the kitchen, run the microwave or dishwasher while he's eating dinner. Give him a treat while the garbage disposal is burping in your sink. Outside, he should hear the lawn mower and leaf blower, and in the bathroom he should listen to the toilet flushing, your electric toothbrush whirring, and your razor buzzing. You want to convey the message to your puppy that none of these sounds is scary or threatening. Be nonchalant about all of these things, and praise the puppy for playing with his toy and not reacting to the noise. Soon he'll pay as little attention to the sounds of your juicer and blender as you do to that mantle clock you never hear chime.

Introduce your Beagle to the family cat or dog slowly, and always supervise any meetings until you're certain that the new pup and the older residents are completely trustworthy. Being hounds, Beagles get along naturally with other dogs and with most other animals—but that doesn't mean that the other animals will enjoy the attentions of your curious Beagle. Keep your puppy in his crate at first and let the older animals sniff him through the crate screen. If both pets seem calm and interested, take the Beagle out of his crate and carefully hold him in your lap. Let the two pets sniff and get to know each other. Don't let them play together unattended until you are sure that they won't harm each other. If the pets don't get along, don't try and force a friendship. Just keep them separated until they get accustomed to and become more tolerant of one another.

The same care should be taken when introducing your new puppy to young children. Teach your children how to hold and pet a puppy. Hold the puppy in your lap and have your children sit in front of you. Calmly let them stroke the puppy's back. Let the kids know that the puppy is not a toy and that they must

Consider the Microchip

In addition to a dog collar and ID tag, think about having your veterinarian insert a microchip in your dog to help find him if he ever gets lost. When scanned, the microchip will show your dog's unique microchip number so that your Beagle can be returned to you as soon as possible. Go to www.akccar.org to learn more about the nonprofit American Kennel Club Companion Animal Recovery (AKC CAR) pet recovery system.

Since 1995, the AKC CAR service has been selected by millions of dog owners who are grateful for the peace of mind and service that AKC CAR offers.

be respectful of the puppy. Set off-limit areas where your children know not to bother the pup, such as in his crate or bed. This will help your puppy feel more confident and safe and create a better relationship between him and all of his family members—big, small, and furry.

At a Glance ...

Your first trip to the pet store may be a little overwhelming. The only supplies you need for your new puppy are a few grooming supplies, a crate, a collar and leash, food dishes, puppy food, and a few toys. Don't overdo it—you'll have plenty of time to stock up on food and treats once you get to know your puppy's likes and dislikes.

. . . .

Don't let your Beagle puppy have free reign of the house. Close doors and set up baby gates and exercise pens to keep your puppy confined to secure, puppy-proofed areas of the house until he is completely house-trained and trustworthy.

. . . .

Introduce your puppy slowly to the many new household sounds around him. The vacuum, dish-washer, laundry, and garbage disposal are all new, scary things to your pup. Take it slow and let your Beagle know that there is nothing to fear from these unfamiliar appliances.

CHAPTER FIVE

Gear Up for Training

Your Beagle's education begins the day he comes into your home. Even if you're not engaging your puppy in actual training sessions, he is still learning from you. Dogs learn primarily by watching your example, so your impressionable pup is taking cues from you even when you're not aware of it. Keep that in mind as you interact with the puppy during his first days at home. When you permit him to sit on your lap, nibble on your fingers, or eat

Introduce your puppy to his leash slowly over a few days' time. Let him get used to the feel of the leash around the house before taking him for his first walk outside.

out of your hand, you're giving him indications about what he's allowed to do and what he's not. A dog's good manners are not taught during formal training sessions, they are learned organically from day-to-day interactions and habitual routines with the dog. It's no coincidence that the best-behaved dogs are owned by dog-smart people who know how to communicate with their dogs.

THE BEAGLE BOND

One of the key components of communicating is trust. There are sonnets, songs, and sculptures praising canine loyalty, and there is no more trusting creature on the planet than a dog. Odds are that you'll gain your Beagle's trust in no time, but that trust is still something you must earn. Luckily, it's not hard to show your puppy that you're trustworthy. You provide the calm security of your home, all those tasty, regular meals, and heartfelt back and neck scratches. Beagles love all those things (especially the tasty food part), and if you're a reliable provider of kibble and love, your Beagle puppy will soon be your most attentive—if not most obedient—friend.

One of your puppy's favorite pastimes is playing, and in fact, all dogs take play very seriously. Playing games is a sure way to bond with your puppy. Be sure you're using safe, soft toys with your pup. Make sure there are no sharp or unsafe parts, such as squeakers, plastic eyes or noses, or stringy stuffing that can become detached from the toy and ingested. Be wary of anything that can be dangerous to the puppy or cause injury. Those puppy teeth are super sharp and can easily rip apart a soft toy, so always thoroughly inspect your Beagle's toys before each play session and supervise your puppy as he plays with his toys.

LET'S PLAY!

Puppy games are a great way to entertain and have fun with your puppy, while at the same time teach him a few basic training lessons. Start with a game plan and a pocketful of tasty dog treats. Keep your games short—three to five minutes—so you don't push his attention span beyond normal puppy limits.

Game 1: Pass the Puppy. This game helps teach the *come* command. With two people sitting on the floor about 10 or 15 feet apart, have one person hold and pet the pup while the other calls to him in a happy voice, "Georgie, come!" Use the puppy's name to reinforce his recognition. When the pup comes running, give him a big hug and a treat. Repeat back and forth several times, but don't overdo it—you don't want your puppy to grow bored with the game and stop responding when his name is called.

For a lively game of fetch, add a tennis ball or favorite small toy, and toss it back and forth for the puppy to retrieve. Beagles have a strong chase instinct and will relish a game of fetch as much as any retriever. When he picks it up, praise and hug him some more, give him a treat to release the toy, and then toss it back to the other person. Repeat back and forth until the puppy gets the idea. Eventually, you will be able to play fetch with your Beagle alone, and he will learn to bring the toy back to you once it is thrown.

Game 2: Hide-and-Seek. This is another fun way to teach the *come* command. Play this game outdoors in your fenced yard or in another safely secured area. When the pup is not looking at you, hide behind a nearby bush or tree. Peek out and watch him as he realizes that you are gone and tries to find you. As soon as he gets close, come out, squat down with arms outstretched, and call him by name, "Monty, come!" You are bonding with your Beagle, using his name and teaching him that he can depend on you to be there when you call.

Game 3: Missing Toy. This game is another favorite because Beagles love to solve problems and seek out lost items. Start by placing one of his favorite toys in plain sight and ask your puppy, "Where is your toy?" and let him take it. Repeat this step several times. Then, while your puppy is safely outside the room, place the toy behind a couch cushion or under a footstool where only part of it shows. Bring him back into the room and ask the same question. Praise him with belly rubs and compliments when he finds it. Repeat this second step several times. Finally, conceal the toy completely and let your puppy sniff it out with that unstoppable hound nose. Trust his nose—he'll soon find his toy and any treats you're hiding in your pockets. Games are terrific teaching forums for your bright, fun-loving Beagle.

Did You Know?

In the late 1800s and early 1900s, more and more Beagle enthusiasts began competing in dog shows and other AKC events. A record seventy-five dogs were entered at the prestigious West-minster Kennel Club dog show in 1917, and it was a Beagle that emerged as the winner of the Hound Group that year. Even more fame came to the breed through field trials, a sport begun in 1890, that has steadily grown over the years into an event for which there are hundreds of clubs throughout the United States, represented in almost all fifty states.

Training Tips

Training your Beagle puppy may take extra patience at times, but follow these simple training tips, and you will see fast results:

1. Use a light, happy tone when training your puppy, and keep your commands short and simple.

2. Stay consistent. Don't let your puppy relax on the couch with you one day, but get angry with him for jumping on the furniture the next.

3. Reward your puppy with a treat or with praise at the moment he does something good (or when he stops doing something bad). You want to reinforce the good deed, not the bad behavior.

4. Never correct your dog for something he did a few minutes earlier. He won't remember what he was doing or understand why you are angry with him.

5. Always stay positive. If you find yourself getting frustrated, stop training for the day and give yourself a break. Training is a lifelong pursuit; don't expect to get it right on day one.

EARLY TRAINING

Whether or not you plan to show your Beagle, it is always a good idea to do a little early obedience training. Both your veterinarian and your groomer will be thankful that your dog will stand calmly on a table while being examined or groomed. It is much easier to deal with a well-behaved dog, and you will be so proud of your clever companion!

Accustom your puppy to wearing a collar and leash, which is a strange experience for such a tiny youngster. Begin by attaching a simple collar, not too tightly, but not so loose that it can get caught on things, causing panic and possible injury. Put it on for a few minutes at a time, lengthening each period until your puppy feels comfortable in his first item of clothing. Don't expect miracles—it may take a few days for your Beagle to get used to wearing it.

Once he is comfortable wearing the collar, attach a small, lightweight leash. The one you select must have a secure buckle, yet be simple enough to attach and release as necessary. Until now, your Beagle has simply gone where he pleased, and he will find it very strange to be attached to someone restricting his movements. For this reason, allow the puppy to lead you for the first few sessions. Once he is used to the feel of the leash, exert a little pressure and begin to lead the way. Now the training can begin in earnest.

When your puppy is ready to venture into the world, begin by taking him to quiet places without too many distractions. His confidence will soon increase and you can begin introducing him to new places with exciting sights, sounds, and smells. He must always be on a secure leash when outside your home. Once you have total confidence in one another, you will be able to let him off leash in certain circumstances, but always keep him in sight, and be sure the place you have chosen for free exercise is safe and enclosed.

Let's hear it for the Beagle! Reinforce house rules throughout your dog's life, and your Beagle will grow into a well-behaved adult.

In the interest of your Beagle's safety and training—and your own sanity—train your puppy to stay in a crate when required. Crates are useful for keeping your puppy confined when you have errands to run or chores to do. Most dogs seem to look upon their crate as a safe place to go and don't mind being confined for short periods of time, which can be helpful, especially for house-training while your Beagle is a puppy.

Take your time when introducing the crate for the first time. Place a soft towel in the crate and toss a few treats inside. Your curious Beagle will give the entire crate (inside and out) a thorough sniff-down. Start by feeding your Beagle a meal or letting him chew on his favorite toy inside the crate. Once he seems comfortable, close the door of the crate for a short while. Remain within sight of your dog and be sure he has a toy or something inside the crate to occupy his mind. To begin with, leave him in the crate for very short intervals—a minute or two is plenty—and gradually build up the time period. After a few days, your Beagle will see his crate as his own personal space, and he will be comfortable

Don't let your puppy nap on the couch one day and then scold him for it the next. Stay consistent and your puppy will more easily understand what is expected of him.

Make Your Puppy a S.T.A.R.

The American Kennel Club has a great program for new puppy owners called the S.T.A.R. Puppy® Program, which is dedicated to rewarding puppies that get off to a good start by completing a basic training class. S.T.A.R. stands for: Socialization, Training, Activity, and Responsibility.

You must enroll in a six-week puppy-training course with an AKC-approved evaluator. When the class is finished, the evaluator will test your puppy on all the training taught during the course, such as being free of aggression toward people and other puppies in the class, tolerating a collar or body harness, allowing his owner to take away a treat or toy, and sitting and coming on command.

If your puppy passes the test, he will receive a certificate and a medal. You and your puppy will also be listed in the AKC S.T.A.R. Puppy records. To learn more about the AKC S.T.A.R. Puppy Program or to find an approved evaluator near you, check out www.akc.org/starpuppy.

inside for hours at a time. However, never confine a dog in a crate for more than a few hours. A good rule of thumb to follow is a three-month-old puppy can be crated during the day for three hours, a four-month-old puppy for four hours, and so forth to a maximum of five or six hours. If you are going to be gone for longer, arrange for a neighbor or family member to stop by and let the puppy out for a potty break and a bit of play time.

OUT ON THE TOWN

Once your puppy starts to feel comfortable around you, your family, and your home, you can begin introducing him to your friends and neighbors. If you have young children, or if others' children visit, always carefully supervise their interactions with your puppy. Youngsters are often attracted to the fun-loving, tail-wagging Beagle, but don't let them assault your dog or toss him about as this may lead to a fear of strangers or an aggressive response to children.

Even though Beagles are generally easygoing, social souls, they still need to have real-life experiences with all kinds of people, including neighbors you see on the street during a walk, children of all ages, men and women in uniform, individuals in wheelchairs, and so forth. Dogs that lack socialization are like people with no social graces or skills, the kind of folk who no one wants to have around. You want your Beagle to be polite, well mannered, and welcome in your friends' homes, just as he is in your home.

When socializing your Beagle out on the town, keep in mind that though your pup may be more than happy to meet the neighborhood German Shepherd, it's possible that the confident guard dog isn't very accepting of strange dogs. Find out about other dogs' temperaments before allowing your Beagle to make friends. Dog owners are usually very forthcoming about their dogs' dislike of other dogs. Once you're certain that the other dog is friendly, introduce the two dogs slowly and with great care. The most important thing for you to do is watch: don't interfere and don't nervously yank on your puppy's leash. Your insecurity and fear will travel right down the leash and your Beagle will immediately sense

Socialize your puppy by introducing him to new people, places, and pets. Approach other dogs with care, and don't force a relationship if either of the two seem unwilling.

Socialization

Socialization is much more than simply having fun with your puppy. Experiencing new places, meeting new people, and hearing loud strange noises help your Beagle mature and gain confidence in himself and the world around him. A Beagle that lacks socialization as a youngster will grow up to be a shy, withdrawn dog that is fearful of new people. Socialization gives your Beagle the opportunity to develop the necessary social graces to become a well-behaved companion.

that something is wrong. If you sense any aggression from either side, back away slowly from the other dog and don't force the interaction. Not all dogs are destined to be fast friends. In most cases, however, your personable Beagle will easily win over the whole neighborhood.

Your Beagle puppy needs a social calendar. Not only are you your Beagle's caregiver, personal trainer, and nutritionist, you're also his cruise director! Set up playdates for your Beagle so he can meet new people and other friendly dogs. Your puppy's calendar should include at least three social outings a week. Take him along with you on your weekend errands. Put him in his crate and tote him along as you pick up your dry cleaning, stop by a friend's house for coffee, or visit a shopping center. The Beagle puppy is portable enough to carry around, and some outdoor cafés allow dogs as do some stores. Of course, most pet stores encourage you to bring your puppy, and what's more fun for your Beagle than visiting a store that has thousands of dog toys on display!

At a Glance ...

The first few months of your puppy's life are the most important. Bond with your Beagle puppy through interactive games that teach him vital lessons such as fetch, hide-and-seek, and coming when called.

Be patient and consistent, and don't get frustrated with your puppy when he doesn't understand right from wrong immediately. Your Beagle is getting used to his new home and the new house rules—which are very different from his instinctive canine pack behaviors.

Show your puppy the world! Introduce him to new places and new people every day. Socialization will help your Beagle puppy grow into a confident, outgoing adult that is a joy to be around.

CHAPTER SIX

House-Training Your Beagle

Beagles have received a bad rap when it comes to house-training, thanks mostly to the legions of impatient, inconsistent owners who've thrown up their hands after a few weeks and said, "I give up!" Beagles are no more challenging to house-train than any other hound with a super-sensitive canine nose. Beagles have noses that provide entirely too much information, noses that make human logic (and our infinitely inferior sense of smell) incomprehensible to dogs.

In fairness to your Beagle, the breed hasn't been considered an indoor companion for that long. The Beagles of yesteryear were kept as hunting dogs, and the pack was never allowed unlimited access to the nobleman's 40-room manor! Packs were kept outdoors, usually in an accessory shelter such as a barn or kennel. It didn't matter where the dogs relieved themselves as they were kept outside for most, if not all, of their lives.

THE RIGHT WAY

Now that dog owners have taken to Beagles as household pets, house-training (controlling where and when a dog relieves himself) is an absolute necessity and a top priority. You'll find that your Beagle will happily adjust to the "good life" and will show no reluctance to house-training—provided you execute house-training the right way.

The right way to house-train a Beagle can be summed up in a few simple words:

• **Crate:** The crate you purchased for your puppy, ideally sized for the adult Beagle, doesn't have any magical properties, but it is an essential tool that will help your Beagle learn house-training rules more quickly and easily.

• **Consistency:** You cannot train your puppy to behave in a certain way without 100 percent consistency. Dogs do not understand exceptions. There are

Always take your puppy to the same spot to relieve himself. Your Beagle will soon realize that this is the one (and only!) spot where he should take care of his business.

Doggy Day Care

If you work full-time and are away from home longer than six hours a day, your Beagle will quickly become bored at home by himself— and boredom leads to unhappiness and destruction. If you don't have any neighbors or family members that can stop by during the day to walk your Beagle or play with him, consider enrolling him in doggy day care. Doggy day care has grown in popularity with full-time working dog owners in the past decade. It is a great way to entertain and socialize your Beagle while you are away from home. Before you find a day care, visit www.dogchannel .com for what to look for in a good facility and tips on interview questions to ask.

rules, and they are black and white. That's how a dog sees and thinks, and that's how you must train your dog. Gray areas are confusing and can wreak havoc in your training efforts.

• **Vigilance:** You can't keep your eyes on your puppy during his every waking moment, but you must try or you'll be stepping over puddles on the kitchen floor for months. Accidents inside the house occur in that one minute you're not watching your puppy. If you have to unload the dishwasher, check your e-mail, or make dinner, put the puppy in his crate.

• **Patience:** House-training doesn't happen overnight. Compared to human babies, puppies learn pretty fast, but it is still going to take at least four to five weeks before you can trust that your Beagle is completely reliable in the house.

CRATE-TRAINING

If you purchased a puppy from a breeder who began house-training for you, follow the method that he or she used. Crate-training is the choice of most breeders, but remember that your house doesn't smell or look like the breeder's house, and the puppy will have to readjust to his new environment. This means that your puppy may lose all of his previous house-training knowledge for the first few days

All-Weather Pal

(or weeks) after you bring him home. For the first few days, limit the puppy's access to one or two rooms (preferably rooms with wood or tile floors that can easily be cleaned). You don't want the puppy getting lost in a spare bedroom while trying to find his way to the backyard. Make it obvious and easy for your little guy. He should be able to get to his "potty place" lickety-split, with nary a second thought. When a puppy has to go, he has to go at that moment. A vigilant, smart owner recognizes the signs and gets the puppy immediately outside.

Like human babies, puppies have virtually no control over their bodily systems. Peeing is like breathing to a pup. He doesn't think about it, which means that it's your job to make him think about it. He doesn't know why you're so obsessed with his body functions, nor understand why you want him to relieve himself in a certain place. House-training is not natural for a puppy, and that's what makes it so difficult for your Beagle to understand.

If you're uneasy about crate-training, you're not thinking like a dog. Dogs consider a crate the best possible place to sleep because it fulfills the two canine requirements for a bed—clean and safe. Dogs instinctively do not like to sleep where they relieve themselves, hence they won't soil their crates. However, if your Beagle's crate is too large, he may go to the bathroom on one side of the crate and sleep on the other. Buy a crate that is large enough to house your Beagle when he is fully grown, but during house-training, block off part of the crate to give your puppy just enough room to stand and turn around in.

Safety is also a concern for dogs, and they usually won't sleep out in the open where a predator (such as the family cat or vacuum) can readily attack them. More likely, your Beagle will choose a corner or space behind a sofa or under a bed rather than the middle of the floor. Without a crate, if your puppy soils his sleeping place, he can simply get up and sleep somewhere else. A puppy can't walk out of a closed crate, so he will intentionally hold his bladder (for as long

At first, carry your Beagle to his potty place when he needs to go outside. He will soon be able to go outside by himself and will let you know when he is finished.

as he can) until you release him to go outside. After a few weeks, your puppy will gain more control over his bladder, and he will be able to hold it for longer and longer periods of time.

A dog crate is a critical accessory for house-training, but don't abuse it. Don't leave a ten-week-old puppy in ___ ____ for eight hours while you're at work and expect the puppy to be d____ ___ _en you get home. He'll be wet and bouncing off the walls of th__ ___ ____ young puppy in the crate for more than a couple hours, un___ ___ _ the pup is three or four months of age, you can increase the l____ __ __ or four hours. No matter the age of the pup, never crate a Beag__ ___ __ ours at a time. If you will be away from home for longer than___ ___ __ a neighbor or dogsitter to stop by and release your puppy for ___ ___ _ some exercise.

Puppies, like all dogs, thrive on h____ ___ ___ they like to know what to expect from day to day. "Crate ti____ ___ _ nap time for a toddler. Crating the puppy midday for a cou__ ___ ___ youngster time to rest and gives you time to catch up on chore__ ___ __ _e puppy is out and about. Naturally, the first thing your pup__ ___ ___ _n waking up is go to the bathroom. In fact, every time you _ ___ ___ _m his crate, whether he was asleep or not, pick him up and ca__ ___ ___ potty break. Once the puppy is a little older, you can lead him ou__ ___ little, pick him up and get him outside as quickly as possible.

During the day, while you are at home to watch him, you ca__ ___ open so that your puppy can come and go as he pleases. You'll see t__ will opt to spend time in his crate on his own. The crate is a great esca__ busy house, a fun place to chew on a favorite toy, and a cool doggy hango__

Learn to recognize your Beagle's bathroom signals. Is he circling the flo__ and sniffing intently? Has he just woken up from a nap? Have you finished a fu__ play session with your pup? In all of these instances, take your puppy outside for

Don't let your puppy get distracted before he's relieved himself. You want your puppy to concentrate and understand the house-training lesson at hand.

⌐ TO OPEN, FOLD AND TEAR HERE ⌐

a potty break. Puppies under twelve weeks of age need to eliminate once every hour—which is about a dozen times a day! Take your Beagle to the same spot outside every time he needs to relieve himself. Use the same phrase each time, such as "go potty" or "get busy." As long as you are consistent, your puppy will learn that these words mean it's time to do his business. Once he goes, let him know he did the right thing by clapping excitedly and giving lots of verbal praise.

Every time you take him outside, use the same pathway and doorway. This will help him remember the quickest way to get outside. In time, your puppy will learn to go to the door and wait, letting you know he needs to go outside. It may take a month or two, but your Beagle will soon get the idea.

Pick a single house-training method and stick with it. Your puppy will get confused if you introduce more than one strategy at a time.

PAPER-TRAINING

Should you consider paper-training your Beagle? Paper-training is usually not intended as a permanent house-training solution, but rather as a transitional step toward outdoor training. However, for owners who live in high-rise apartments with little or no outdoor access or owners who work long hours away from home, paper-training is a reasonable approach.

Choose a room that has a wood or tile floor that is easy to clean and that is close to where the family spends the most time. Use baby gates or an exercise pen to cordon off the area so that the puppy is confined within the room. Cover the entire floor of the area with newspaper or puppy pads. Place your Beagle's crate or bed, his food and water dishes, and a few chew toys in the area as well so that

Clean up after your puppy with a nontoxic household cleaner with pet-odor removal. If your puppy can smell his scent in the carpet, he is more likely to relieve himself in those spots again and again.

A PIECE OF HISTORY

The American-English Beagle Club was founded in 1884, the same year as the American Kennel Club. A second Beagle club, the National Beagle Club, came along in 1888, the year it held the first ever field trial for Beagles, and its purpose was to hold field trials and improve the breed's performance in the field. Eventually the two clubs merged to become the National Beagle Club of America, the current parent club of the breed. The National Beagle Club of America continued to govern Beagle field trials until 1936 when the responsibilities were handed over to the Beagle Advisory Committee established by the AKC.

Get to know your puppy's potty signals and keep a strict house-training schedule. Take your puppy outside after all naps, meals, and play sessions, and you will avoid excess accidents around the house.

he has something to keep him occupied. Put your Beagle in this area whenever you are unable to keep an eye on him.

After a few days, you'll notice that your puppy is relieving himself in one general area. One piece at a time, remove the newspaper or puppy pads from around your Beagle's chosen potty spot until he is consistently relieving himself on one piece of paper. If he slips up and goes off the paper, simply add another piece of paper until he starts going on the paper once again. It is a slow process, but soon your Beagle will realize that the paper is where he is supposed to go.

Once he is consistently going on the single piece of paper, remove the baby gates or exercise pen, and slowly move the piece of paper where you would like him to start going permanently. Move the sheet only a few inches each day so that your puppy doesn't get confused. If you eventually want your puppy to start going outside, move the paper toward the door you most commonly use to go outside. Place a thickness of five or six sheets of newspaper or a puppy pad by the door so that the dog learns to associate the location of the paper with going outside. When the puppy relieves himself on the paper, cheer for him wholeheartedly! Praising the puppy lets him know he did something important, and he will want to repeat the behavior so that he can be praised again and again. Of course, if outdoor house-training is your goal, it's best to carry him outside immediately when he shows any signs of having to go to the bathroom (unless that means a ten-floor elevator ride). With vigilance and consistency, your puppy will learn that the paper is where he should do his business, and you can eventually begin taking him outside to go potty as well.

ACCIDENTS WILL HAPPEN

Accidents occur because owners aren't paying attention, and usually by the time the puppy is giving his owner a sign that he needs to go, it's too late. You may have only ten to fifteen seconds from the moment he starts to sniff around the floor, wiggle his little Beagle behind, or whimper. As the puppy gets older, his signaling starts earlier and he'll become more reliable.

But, no matter how consistent, patient, and vigilant you are, accidents will happen. If you catch the puppy in the act, make a loud noise and immediately pick him up and carry him to his outdoor spot (or newspaper). Always praise him when he does his business in the right place. If you discover an accident in the house, bite your tongue and grab the deodorizer. If you don't catch him in the act, it is senseless to correct the dog. Your puppy will have no idea what you're belly-aching about, and he will simply assume it has nothing to do with him.

Be sure you clean up the mess thoroughly with a nontoxic household cleaner with pet-odor remover. You must completely remove the scent so that your über-sniffing hound can't find it. Just as he uses the same potty spot outside, he will continue to relieve himself in the same spot inside if you don't clean it up thoroughly. Pet-supply stores sell excellent odor removers: choose one that's organic and green. Never use a household cleaner that can be toxic to dogs.

At a Glance ...

No matter which house-training method you choose to train your Beagle, consistency, vigilance, and patience are key. House-training will be confusing for your Beagle at first, but with good habits and positive reinforcement, your puppy will be house-trained in no time.

. . . .

Crate-training is the most reliable and trusted method of house-training. Crate-training combines the puppy's need of a secure, protected sleeping area and his instinctual desire to keep his sleeping area clean.

. . . .

Your Beagle will have accidents in the house, but there is no sense in correcting your puppy unless you catch him in the act. If it has been more than five seconds since the accident, simply clean up the spot and vow to be more vigilant in the future.

CHAPTER SEVEN

Basic Beagle Obedience

Like smart kids, Beagles bore easily. They are free-thinking, independent hounds that believe they can solve problems on their own, which can make training challenging for even the most patient owner. Of course, no two dogs are exactly the same. Your Beagle may be a happy follower or you may have a smarter-than-normal Beagle that has figured out how to unlatch the safety bolt on your fence or get into even the most remote garbage containers. Based

on the personality and drive of your Beagle, you must find the best way to train him. You may be able to keep his focus for a good ten-minute lesson or he may be off chasing butterflies after just thirty seconds.

Where dogs are concerned, lessons can be tedious and boring, especially long classes with endless repetition and no snack breaks. Beagles are bright, eager hounds that look forward to happy, fun times spent with you, his favorite human. Keep all training sessions with your Beagle brisk, treat-filled, and positive.

Getting and keeping your Beagle's attention is step one (and the most important step) in training. Most likely, food rewards—small cubes of cheese or pieces of a favorite treat—will be all the incentive your chowhound needs to pay attention. Don't tease your dog or ramp up his excitement with the treats. Offer a food reward only for a job well done. And don't overdo the treats—a little liver goes a long way! Fill his nose and his mind, not his stomach. As long as treats are used in moderation, they are the perfect motivators for the eternally hungry Beagle.

When introducing basic obedience commands like *sit*, *down*, and *stay*, use food rewards. As you practice the lessons, don't offer a treat every time your dog obeys. Instead, offer different rewards: a treat, a pat, or a "good boy." Be unpredictable so that your dog can't anticipate your every move. You'll keep him interested and at the same time slowly wean him off the food treats. Once the dog is fully trained, he will obey commands with only your verbal approval as a reward. Keep your training sessions short and sweet. Never train when you're in a cranky mood after a long day's work. Dogs will pick up on your bad mood, which is readable in your body language and tone of voice.

If your Beagle is having trouble mastering the *sit* command, gently press on his hindquarters as you say "sit," guiding him into position. This will help him understand what you are asking of him.

SIT

The *sit* command is a natural starting point because it's relatively simple to get a dog to sit, even a distracted, young dog like your Beagle puppy. Begin by finding a nice, quiet location indoors to practice, free from distractions. Attach a leash on your Beagle's collar. Hold the food reward in your right hand and the leash in your left hand. Allow the Beagle to sniff the treat, but don't let him take it from you. Now that you have his attention, move the treat up and over his head as you say "sit" in a stern voice. As you raise the treat, he will follow it and his hindquarters will magically descend. *Sit*, voilà! If your Beagle doesn't sit when looking up, place your hand on his hindquarters and gently press down as you lower the treat. That usually does the trick. The act is not intentional at first, so you must say "good, sit" as soon as he assumes the position. Repeat the lesson a few times every day. Within a few days, your Beagle will make the connection between your command and the action.

COME

The *come* command is the most important command you will teach your dog. Beagles love to run—fast and in whichever direction strikes their fancy at the moment. Experienced Beagle owners know that teaching the *come* command is challenging, but not nearly as difficult as recalling a runaway Beagle. Make sure your dog has this lesson ingrained into his Beagle brain—you may end up using the *come* command to get your Beagle out of dangerous or life-threatening situations.

Begin this exercise using food rewards. When your Beagle hears you say, "Benny, come" what he's really hearing is, "Benny, come and get it!" Yes, you are bribing your dog with treats. Bribery is one way of looking at reward-based training, but often a tasty reward is necessary, particularly when you're dealing with a Beagle whose every waking thought is led by his nose and stomach. Eventually, you will wean your dog off food rewards for this lesson. Alternate food rewards with verbal praise and belly rubs. In time, your Beagle will run to you joyously whether you have a treat in your hand or not. A reliable recall is the most important thing you'll teach your dog, and you should put as much energy into the *come* command as you do into house-training or leash training.

To teach the *come* command, attach a long leash to his collar and choose a quiet area of the house. Kneel down a few feet from the puppy, open your arms wide, and say, "Benny, come" in a happy, inviting voice. As he starts running toward you, give him lots of verbal praise, and when he reaches you, give him lots of pets and a treat. You shouldn't have to tug on the leash. The leash is only attached to keep him focused on the exercise at hand. Practice this routine for as long as it takes for him to respond consistently. Once you're satisfied that he will run to you when called, practice without the leash, but stay in a distraction-free area of the house.

When you're ready to practice this exercise outside, be sure that you're working within a securely fenced area. Never risk losing your dog: if you're not in a secure area, keep the dog on a leash. Even if you live in a quiet neighborhood, your Beagle still will hear birds chirping, small animals rustling in the distance, and the wind. He will be easily distracted, but this is a good environment in which to reinforce the *come* lesson. Again, place your Beagle in the sit position, and move a few feet in front of him. Call him to you. Keep practicing this lesson from farther and farther away until you're sure that no matter what the distraction, your Beagle will come to you when called.

How often should you practice the *come* command? At most, only two or three times a day. You don't want your Beagle to get bored with this exercise. Save the *come* lesson for a moment when you've got time to bond with your dog or when you've got a particularly delicious treat.

DOWN

The easiest way to teach the *down* command is as an extension of the sit. Once you have the dog in the sit position, hold the treat in front of him and lower the treat toward the floor. Slide the treat along the floor away from his nose as you say "down." Don't give him the treat unless he assumes a down position with his chest and tummy on the floor. Try it a few times without touching him. If he still refuses to assume the down position after a few tries, gently slide his front legs out in front of him to show him what you want. Try not

to touch his paws (most dogs dislike anyone touching their feet), but rather, hold his upper arms. When he assumes the correct position (with his elbows on the floor), give him the treat and calmly say "good, down." Avoid giving him wildly happy praise, as he may think you're releasing him. As you practice this exercise, gradually increase the length of time the dog stays in the down position. If you can get a puppy to stay in the down position for ten seconds, you're on your way to obedience trials!

Be especially sensitive when teaching the *down* command. Dogs enjoy lying down on their own, but they do not like being forced into a position that they perceive as submissive. No matter how unresponsive your Beagle is, never press down on his shoulders or physically force him to lie down. This kind of coercion is counterproductive and may make the dog fearful or resentful.

STAY

Beagles are largely unimpressed by this command because they believe that when you say "stay," you're really saying "stay right there while I think of what we should do next." In truth, stay is the period of time that passes until you say "OK" and release your Beagle from his sit, stand, or down position. It doesn't take much practice to teach a dog to do nothing, which is essentially what you're asking your dog to do when you say, "Lola, stay."

You can teach your Beagle to stay in any position, though sit or down is the best starting point. To begin, place the dog's leash on his collar and find a treat. With the lead in your left hand and the treat in your right hand, say "stay" while standing directly in front of the dog. Silently count to five and then step to the side of the dog. Say "OK," and give the dog the treat and a pat.

For the first week, practice the *stay* command, and once he's doing it reliably, gradually increase the distance between you. Hold your hand up, with your palm facing the dog, indicating that he must stay until you release him. Soon you will be able to cue your dog to stay with only the hand signal, and your Beagle will stay for longer periods of time. Praise and treat the dog after he completes each lesson, but eventually replace the treats with only verbal praise.

The Universal OK

The universal word, "OK," speaks to dogs and humans in all languages. In dog speak, it means "OK, you're done"; in other words, it's a release command. After you've completed an exercise, say "OK," and engage the dog in some other activity or let him have free time to play. You can also use the word before you let the dog out of his crate or out the back door. When you open the crate or the door, say "OK," which will signal him to move. With a wandering breed like the Beagle, it's always good to be in control of your dog when there's an open door nearby.

Can Your Dog Pass the Canine Good Citizen® Test?

An AMERICAN KENNEL CLUB Program

Once your Beagle is ready for advanced training, you can start training him for the American Kennel Club Canine Good Citizen® Program. This program is for dogs that are trained to behave at home, out in the neighborhood, and in the city. It's easy and fun to do. Once your dog learns basic obedience and good canine manners, a CGC evaluator gives your dog ten basic tests. If he passes, he's awarded a Canine Good Citizen® certificate. Many trainers offer classes with the test as the final to graduate from the class. To find an evaluator in your area, go to www.akc.org/events/cgc/cgc_bystate.cfm.

Many therapy dogs and guide dogs are required to pass the Canine Good Citizen® test in order to help as working and service dogs in the community. There are ten specific skills that a dog must master in order to pass the Canine Good Citizen® test:

1. Let a friendly stranger approach and talk to his owner
2. Let a friendly stranger pet him
3. Be comfortable being groomed and examined by a friendly stranger
4. Walk on a leash and show that he is in control and not overly excited
5. Move through a crowd politely and confidently
6. Sit and stay on command
7. Come when called
8. Behave calmly around another dog
9. Not bark at or react to a surprise distraction
10. Show that he can be left with a trusted person away from his owner

In order to help your dog pass the AKC CGC test, first enroll him in basic training classes or a CGC training class. You can find classes and trainers near you by searching the AKC website. When you feel that your Beagle is ready to take the test, locate an AKC-approved CGC evaluator to set up a test date, or sign up for a test that is held at a local AKC dog show or training class. For more information about the AKC Canine Good Citizen® Program, visit www.akc.org /events.cgc.

HEEL

The term *heel* is obedience-trial language for when a dog walks alongside his owner's left leg (technically, his left heel) under complete control, matching the owner's precise speed, without pulling ahead or falling behind. Every time the owner stops, the dog sits automatically.

OK, wake up. There's a ten-week-old Beagle dancing around your kitchen because he loves racing you around the block every time he sees you pick up his leash! The goal for your Beagle puppy shouldn't be a perfect heel, but rather, a calm, controlled walk around the block. It's no fun being pulled down the street by a Beagle that thinks it's a race every time you say the magic "W" word.

Beagles will approach a walk with great enthusiasm—it's the closest thing they have to a hare chase! Don't let your Beagle think that you're a dull walking companion. Don't start at a tortoise's pace when your Beagle thinks he's in it for hare. Put the leash on his collar, keep the dog to your left side, and walk at a good, quick pace. He will keep up with you and focus straight ahead. Keeping a good pace will help keep the Beagle's nose up, too. Every scenthound views a walk as an opportunity to sniff the neighborhood and uncover an adventure. That's a big distraction, and your quiet walk may not be as exciting.

Bring along a handful of treats, and keep them in your left hand. If your hungry Beagle thinks that hand is going to give him goodies, he will stay close to your side and not pull forward. Let him smell the treat in your hand, and every ten steps or so, give him a little nibble if he's walking nicely. Keep the leash taut to keep your Beagle going in your direction, but avoid yanking on the leash even if he's pulling ahead or not walking politely. If he's misbehaving, hold the leash firmly and ignore him or simply change directions. Go left when he's pulling forward, or stop in your tracks completely. Keep him on his toes and let him know that you're the leader, the one who decides which direction you're going, when you start and stop, and when he gets a treat. Some Beagles are incurable pullers, and a collar may not be the best option. Look into a halter or harness that affords the owner more control over the dog.

Be the Leader

Your Beagle considers himself part of your family pack. By training your Beagle and providing firm house rules for him to follow, you will establish yourself as the pack leader, and therefore, your Beagle's alpha and primary teacher. While your puppy is young, have only one person train him and teach him commands. This will ensure that each lesson is taught consistently and will help to avoid confusion for your puppy.

Puppies don't need to learn a perfect heel, but practicing good manners while walking on a leash is a good lesson for every dog to learn.

Hounds of the Chase

Beagles and other foxhounds were bred to chase rabbits and foxes. It's in their makeup to want to run after moving objects. One way to focus on that instinct is to let your puppy chase you. Attach the leash to his collar, and encourage the puppy to run after you. In a happy, fun voice say, "Come and get me!" Never turn the tables on your Beagle and chase him. You don't want him to think that it's fun or acceptable to run away from you.

TAKE IT AND LEAVE IT

Your Beagle's insatiable appetite and curious nose will likely get him into trouble sooner rather than later. The *take it* and *leave it* commands will help you control your Beagle when he wraps his furry lips around something he shouldn't, such as the kitchen trash, a couch pillow, or more seriously, a poisonous plant or discarded piece of food on the sidewalk.

First, you must help your Beagle understand the meaning of *take it*. Hold a treat in the palm of your right hand, and offer it to your dog. When he sniffs the treat and tries to take it, close your fingers around the treat so that he can't reach it. Be prepared for your Beagle to paw and cry and lick at your hand. Wait patiently while he settles down. Once he is calm, open your hand and say "take it" as he eats the treat. Keep repeating this exercise until your Beagle calmly waits for your cue to take the treat.

Once your Beagle learns the meaning of *take it*, you can start teaching him the basics of *leave it*, which will be a little bit more difficult for your Beagle to master. Again, place a treat in the palm of your right hand and offer it to your Beagle. When he tries to take the treat, say "leave it," and close your fingers around the treat. Once he settles, open your hand and say "take it." Repeat this exercise two or three times a day until your Beagle starts to get the idea.

When you think your Beagle knows the meaning of *take it* and *leave it*, and he consistently takes and leaves the treats at your words, you can try and use the commands in real-world situations. Take your Beagle for his daily walk, but place a few toys and treats along your usual route. When your Beagle sniffs out a treat or toy (you know he will!), say "leave it," and keep walking past the item. Don't stop or hesitate. Your Beagle should quickly refocus his attention on the walk at hand. Practice this a few times each day when out walking—but be sure to practice *take it* on your walks as well. You don't want your Beagle to get frustrated!

HIGHER EDUCATION

Learning basic obedience commands is just the beginning of your Beagle's training. Continue your Beagle's education with training classes taught by professional dog trainers. Find local puppy- and dog-training classes through your veterinarian, pet-supply store, or through your local Beagle breed club. Find your local breed club by visiting the AKC website at www.akc.org or the National Beagle Club of America website at http://clubs.akc.org/NBC.

Sometimes it may take a professional to help train your rambunctious Beagle. If you are frustrated with your training efforts, don't hesitate to ask for some extra help. Ask your veterinarian, breeder, or local Beagle club for professional-dog-trainer recommendations. You can also find a list of certified trainers through a few online organizations, including the Association of Pet Dog Trainers (www.apdt.com) or the Certification Council for Professional Dog Trainers (www.ccpdt.org). Be sure that the trainer you choose has been certified by the CCPDT. Trainers must continue to educate themselves in the latest dog-training techniques and equipment in order to stay certified.

Never stop training your Beagle and practicing the basic commands. He'll enjoy the attention and you'll be proud of the results.

At a Glance ...

Patience, consistency, and positive reinforcement are key to successful dog training. Keep your training sessions short, sweet, and full of tasty treats—your energetic Beagle has a short attention span!

Start with the basic obedience commands—*sit, stay, down, come, heel, take it*, and *leave it*—and then graduate to more difficult lessons. Review each lesson a few times each day, but don't overdo it. You don't want your Beagle to get bored or frustrated.

Seek out professional support through training classes or dog trainers. Visit the AKC website at www.akc.org or the National Beagle Club of America website at http://clubs.akc.org/NBC for more information on your local Beagle club and courses near you.

CHAPTER EIGHT

A Nose for Nutrition

Beagles are always hungry, even when they're eating. Unlike many dogs, Beagles will not stop eating once they're full. It's been suggested that the feeling of "full" has never been documented in a single Beagle. For some Beagles, eating is more than their favorite hobby—it's an occupation, an obsession, a reason for waking up. The only joy and excitement that compare to the sight of a rabbit in flight is the succulent image of a bowl of rabbit stew!

Anyone who's lived with a Beagle instantly recognizes the truth in all this chowhound talk, but more importantly it's a message for responsible owners. If not closely monitored, the Beagle's healthy appetite will quickly lead to obesity—that bottomless stomach will become a giant pot belly before you know it!

Obesity in Beagles is no joke. This is a little dog, and even five extra pounds on his small frame makes a big difference. It's fair to say that any dog with a voracious appetite, regardless of breed, is more prone to weight problems than a dog with a normal appetite. Owners should strive to keep their Beagles lean, controlling their dogs' portions at mealtimes and limiting treats and snacks (especially on lazy or less active days).

Your breeder will likely advise you about a feeding schedule. New puppies, ages eight to twelve weeks, will need to be fed as frequently as four times a day. Little bellies can only handle little meals. Once the puppy is three months old,

Beagles are chowhounds to the core. Monitor your dog's weight through measured portions and regularly scheduled feedings.

feed him three times a day (breakfast, lunch, and dinner); and by six months, feed him twice a day, instead offering a nutritious snack at lunchtime. Some owners feed their adult dogs only once a day, but because Beagles prefer to eat in the morning and the evening, it's best to divide their daily portion in half. The twice-a-day rule is good to follow for all small dogs like the Beagle.

HOW TO CHOOSE

Although it may not seem like it as your Beagle devours his food at mealtimes, it requires a surprisingly small amount of food to keep an active Beagle healthy and satisfied. Only a high-quality dog food can sustain an active dog in limited portions, and your Beagle will be glad that you're buying the best possible food for him. How do you select the best high-quality food for your Beagle? Many dog owners will advise you to go with the brand of food that your dog likes the best. Beagles aren't fussy and will likely gobble down any dog food with gusto, so don't take that advice too seriously. The best starting point is to find out which brand of food your breeder feeds his or her dogs or which brand your veterinarian recommends for your Beagle based on his age and lifestyle.

Browsing the dog-food aisles at a pet store will give you a lot of information, most likely more than you need. There are dozens of brands, each of which offer

Natural Alternatives

Dog owners are often tempted to try many of the new innovations they find at their favorite pet-supply stores. One of the newer products is natural dog food, sold in the refrigerated section. These natural dog foods are made of high-quality meats and fish, with natural preservatives and minimal processing. Look for these specialty foods with higher percentages of chicken, lamb, or fish, without grains, starches, and other fillers, boasting added antioxidants and Omega fatty acids. More easily digestible than other foods, these natural foods are recommended for older or recuperating dogs as well as for pregnant females and dogs with grain sensitivity or skin or digestive problems.

Changing Diets

If you plan on changing your Beagle's diet, do so slowly. A quick change could make him sick. Mix small amounts of the new food with the old food over a few days, gradually adding more of the new food and less of the old food until a complete change has been made. This will help your dog get accustomed to the change without disrupting his normal habits.

many different flavors and formulas. Begin your quest by reading the ingredients label on a few different packages. The ingredients are listed by weight:

• The first ingredient on the list should be a high-quality meat such as chicken, beef, lamb, or turkey. Chicken meal (or lamb meal, turkey meal, etc.) may be listed as a second ingredient, but "meal by-products" or "meat meal" should not. "Meal" is a term used for a dried form of ground protein that is not natural or healthy for your pup.

• Many dog foods contain grains, and some companies aren't shy about naming that grain in the flavor, such as "turkey and barley" or "chicken and brown rice." While grains aren't essential components of a dog's diet, quality grains such as barley, rice, and oats are perfectly healthy for dogs. Avoid dog foods that include fillers such as rice hulls, soybean meal, or corn bran.

• Ideally, you're looking for a product that has no artificial colors, flavors, sweeteners, or preservatives. Abbreviations and long, complicated words are likely preservatives, such as BHT, BHA, ethoxyquin, and sodium metabisulphite. Be on the lookout for menadione, also commonly called vitamin K3 or dimethyl-primidinol sulfate (or sulfite). This is a synthetic version of vitamin K that is banned for human use by the FDA. Natural preservatives such as tocopherols (vitamin E) and ascorbic acid (vitamin C) are what you should see instead.

• It's a plus if you see vegetables on the list, as well as fruits. Carrots, peas, pumpkin, and sweet potatoes are popular veggies used in quality dog foods, and apples and blueberries top the list of fruits.

• Dog foods that are labeled "complete and balanced" must meet the standards set forth by the Association of American Feed Control Officials (AAFCO). Choosing a dog food with a "complete and balanced" rating will help you relax knowing that the nutrition in the food is sound.

LIFESTAGE FORMULAS

Most dog-food brands are also offered in a variety of lifestage formulas. Just as human babies require a very different diet than adults or seniors, puppies also require a different diet than adult or senior Beagles. Choose a lifestage formula based on your Beagle's age, lifestyle, and weight. If your Beagle is primarily an inside dog that does not take regular walks

A PIECE OF HISTORY

Imported from Britain's most celebrated packs, Beagles came to the United States around 1860 and were used for hunting in braces (pairs) and packs. In 1884, the breed was accepted by the American Kennel Club and competed in the Sporting Group until 1929. The breed was moved to the newly formed Hound Group in 1930 where it remains today.

You won't be surprised to learn that Beagles aren't good candidates for free-feeding. They have too voracious an appetite to leave dried food out all day, which is commonly done with many dogs. Beagles don't nibble their kibble—they swallow it and look for more. Always leave fresh water out for your dog, especially if you're feeding mainly a dried kibble.

or run around the house all day, he may require a different formula than that of a full-time field Beagle. If you feel that your dog is not getting the nutrition he needs from his current diet, discuss alternatives with your veterinarian, breeder, or a veterinary nutritionist.

Puppy Formulas

Puppy food is fortified with extra protein and fat to help sustain your growing pup. In their first year, puppies grow incredibly fast, and their excess energy and quick metabolism burn off fat and calories almost as fast as your Beagle can eat. To be labeled "complete and balanced" by the AAFCO, puppy food must have at least 20 percent protein and 8 percent fat, plus essential minerals and vitamins to support growth and bone development. With the help of your breeder or veterinarian, choose a puppy food that will support your Beagle's growth throughout his first year, and be sure to feed him at regular intervals during the day. Once he is a year old, you can slowly transition him to an adult food that is formulated for weight maintenance rather than growth.

Beagles over seven or eight years old are considered seniors, but every dog ages differently. If you notice your Beagle is gaining weight, discuss changing his diet with your vet.

Adult and Senior Formulas

At about twelve months of age, your Beagle's bones and muscles have matured, and he has basically reached his full adult size. In order to maintain a healthy body weight, he needs a food with a more reserved amount of protein and fat. According to AAFCO standards, the protein and fat requirements for adult food formulas are slightly less than puppy food: 18 percent protein and 5 percent fat. Gradually switch to an adult formula around your Beagle's first birthday, and determine your dog's serving size by evaluating his current weight and activity level. Continue to feed him twice a day, splitting his normal daily serving into two meals.

In recent years, pet-food manufacturers have released more and more food formulas for the senior dog and for dogs with allergies or sensitivities to certain types of meat or grain. As your Beagle gets older, you'll notice that his energy level will start to lessen and he will sleep more and play less. In order to maintain a healthy weight, your Beagle will need even less protein and fat in his diet, but his food should be fortified with extra vitamins and nutrients. Some senior foods even come in smaller bite sizes that are easier to chew for senior dogs with sensitive teeth or gums. If you notice that your senior Beagle is gaining or losing weight, talk to your veterinarian about different food options. Your vet will help you decide on a food and feeding schedule that are best for your Beagle based on his age and eating habits.

A QUESTION OF TASTE

The most common types of dog food are dry kibble (which comes in bags or sacks), wet (cans or plastic containers), and semi-moist (pouches), all of which are popular with Beagles. Your choice will depend on your Beagle's age, health, activity level, and quite possibly, his taste buds.

Dry (kibble): Most Beagle owners use kibble as their dog's primary food source due to its economical price, long shelf life, and easy cleanup. Veterinarians recommend dry food because of its ability to scrape and clean a dog's teeth of plaque and tartar buildup as he chews. It is easily measured and easily digestible—both of which will help your Beagle maintain a consistent weight throughout his life. If your Beagle inhales his food or is a picky eater, add a splash of warm water or low-sodium, low-fat chicken broth to his bowl. This will help soften the food and act as a fragrant incentive to eat.

Wet (canned): Wet food is the most expensive food choice, but your Beagle is certain to enjoy the tastiest cuts of meat and ample gravy that is included in each can. Most canned foods contain about 70 percent water, which will keep your Beagle hydrated, but it may also cause digestive problems or diarrhea due to its richness. Many owners mix a scoop or two of wet food into their Beagle's bowl of dry food at mealtimes. This gives your Beagle the best of both worlds: a basis of kibble for nutrition with a dash of flavor to moisten the meal.

Semi-moist: Semi-moist food should be reserved for only the pickiest of eaters, as this tasty, soft food is often loaded with preservatives and sweeteners. These additives may cause weight gain in your Beagle or result in unhealthy teeth and gums. However, veterinarians may recommend semi-moist food for senior dogs with sensitive teeth and gums or a low body weight. Be sure to check the ingredient label on any food before buying, and consult your veterinarian if you have any questions about food choice or diet changes for your Beagle.

Not all Beagles will eat anything put in their bowls. For picky eaters, try adding a few choice cooked veggies or lean meats in with their kibble to tempt their taste buds.

HOME COOKING

There's no doubt that your Beagle will love anything you prepare for him in the kitchen. A home-cooked diet is an alternative choice for extremely picky eaters or for dogs that are allergic to any of the basic ingredients used in commercial dog foods. But keep in mind that taking on a home-cooked diet for your Beagle is

Water

You should always have at least two bowls of fresh, cool water available at all times for your Beagle—one inside the house and one outside. Water helps disseminate nutrients throughout your dog's body and flush away the excess waste. Be sure to check the water dishes daily and refill them when necessary.

Be sure to take fresh water with you on all of your walks and activities with your Beagle. Keep him well hydrated and take occasional breaks, especially on hot days.

not a simple task. Cooking for your Beagle means more than just frying up some ground turkey or chicken and placing it in your dog's food bowl. Though your Beagle will probably still eat this plain fare with gusto, a complete and balanced diet will include an assortment of whole ingredients from chicken to beef to potatoes, rice, and vegetables. You will have to research canine nutrition and work closely with your vet to keep track of safe ingredients for your dog and maintain a healthy balance of vitamins and nutrients in his everyday diet.

WHAT TO AVOID

Every Beagle's favorite time of day is suppertime, and that includes your suppertime, too. The canine world's most gifted beggar, the Beagle will use his soulful eyes and pathetic glances to win over your last pork chop. Keep your Beagle's waist and good health in mind before tossing him a leftover scrap or emptying your dinner plate in his bowl. Be cautious with human foods that can be toxic to dogs. That list is topped by chocolate—the darker the chocolate, the worse for your Beagle. In addition to chocolate, the ASPCA warns dog owners to avoid these human foods: coffee, avocados, macadamia nuts, grapes, raisins, yeast dough, onions, garlic, and chives. While no Beagle will pass up a lick of your ice cream cone, dogs shouldn't be offered milk either because dogs lack sufficient amounts of the enzyme lactase in their systems to break down the lactose. Consuming milk or milk products may result in an upset stomach or diarrhea.

AFTER-DINNER SNACKS

Be creative with your Beagle's special treats! You can choose low-calorie treats to keep your Beagle happy. Kids know that baby carrots aren't as good as chocolate chip cookies, but your Beagle will get very excited when you present him with a frozen carrot to gnaw on. Rouse your Beagle's chase instincts by having him catch popcorn (hold the butter and salt) or unsweetened breakfast cereal. You may find

It's best never to feed your Beagle table scraps, but if you decide to give your dog some healthy human snacks such as carrots or plain popcorn, place them in his dish for him to enjoy.

your Beagle is fond of certain fruits, even ones that you wouldn't expect a dog to like. Slices of apples and pears are crisp and worth a crunch, and some dogs love bananas and even grapefruit. (Remember to avoid grapes!) Try celery, green beans, or snap peas, and if your dog isn't fond of veggies, smear a little peanut butter on them and try again. The same works for apples and bananas. A good rule of thumb with vegetables is to only offer your dog veggies that you would eat raw. Avoid raw potatoes, winter squashes, Brussels sprouts, and so forth.

At a Glance ...

Choosing a dog-food brand and formula can be overwhelming. Select a food based on your Beagle's age, weight, activity level, and taste. Talk with your vet about portion size and feeding schedules to find the right balance for your Beagle's individual needs.

. . . .

If your Beagle is a picky eater or if he is allergic to the basic ingredients of commercial dog food, an alternative diet of natural ingredients or even a home-cooked diet may be for you. Natural formulas contain fresh products with minimal processing or preservatives that may interfere with your Beagle's sensitive digestive system.

. . . .

Dog treats purchased at your local pet superstore are high in fat and preservatives, which may lead to a pudgy Beagle. Try some healthy human-snack alternatives, such as small pieces of baked chicken, unsalted popcorn, or frozen veggies. You'd be surprised what your Beagle's taste buds desire.

Grooming Your Beagle

All Beagle owners want their dogs to look handsome, and with this breed, grooming is easy. Because Beagles love to play outdoors and work hard, some owners recommend bathing them weekly, though for most suburban owners, monthly will do just fine. Nonetheless, soaping up a little Beagle takes a lot less time and energy than bathing a Golden Retriever or Yorkshire Terrier, so don't feel overwhelmed. Regardless of your dog's lifestyle,

regular brushing will help to keep the coat clean between baths, and a quick daily once-over will keep your Beagle looking healthy and clean.

It's important to introduce regular grooming habits while your Beagle is still a young puppy. From the first day you bring your puppy home, begin running your hands all over his body, including his face, in his ears, over his belly, and around his feet and toes. This will desensitize him to your touch and help him stay calm and comfortable as you brush and bathe him during your grooming sessions. In time, your Beagle will come to love grooming sessions because it means spending one-on-one time with his favorite human—you!

BRUSHING THE COAT

The Beagle's medium-length coat is both smooth and hard. The majority of the year, Beagles will drop their short hairs here and there around the house, but twice a year—in the spring and the fall—they undergo a heavy shed. Most Beagle owners think very little about grooming, but weekly brushing and monthly bathing will help remove loose fur and keep the coat healthy and shiny.

Beagles are wash-and-wear hounds, and they don't mind getting dirty! Fortunately, the breed tends to be pretty tidy and will self-groom regularly. Groom your Beagle on the floor or on a table with a nonslip surface. Some owners find that a table is more comfortable than squatting or sitting on the floor. If you use the floor, don't bend over the dog to brush his coat, as this is a threatening position that will make your dog uneasy and uncomfortable. Before brushing, run a stainless steel comb gently through your Beagle's coat to remove any shed hair or

As your Beagle's coat thickens in the fall and thins in the spring, he will undergo a surprisingly heavy shed. Keep dropped hairs to a minimum by brushing your Beagle daily during shedding seasons.

Start clipping your puppy's nails and massaging his feet at a young age. With the help of a few treats, your Beagle will learn to tolerate (and even enjoy!) a monthly pedicure.

Did You Know?

Dog owners often overlook the chore of brushing their Beagle's teeth. Studies show that 80 percent of dogs show signs of oral disease as early as age three. Poor dental health affects more than just your Beagle's teeth and gums. Oral infection and tooth decay can spread to your dog's kidneys, liver, and even his heart. So pick up that tube of doggy toothpaste and start brushing!

dirt. Some owners skip the comb and simply use a grooming mitt or hound glove to remove hair and dirt and to stimulate the skin and coat. The grooming mitt is also a nice way to give your dog a quick massage.

Begin brushing the Beagle from his head toward his rear, never too vigorously, but with enough energy to work all the way down to the skin. Be careful not to scrape his skin and be extra careful when you're brushing under his belly, inside his legs, and around his face. Alternate brushing with and against the grain of his coat, which will help loosen any dead hair that may be hiding deep within your Beagle's coat. Brushing weekly will help stimulate your Beagle's skin and coat growth and will shorten the length of his shedding seasons. Give your vacuum a much-needed rest, and brush out as much shed hair as you can during your weekly grooming duties.

Beagles have a double coat with an insulating bottom layer and a harder, thicker outer layer. Their hair can get quite greasy, so a monthly bath is a must.

THE BEAGLE'S BATH

Contrary to popular belief, bathing does not remove all the essential oils from your dog's coat. Regular bathing removes dirt and odors and keeps the coat looking shiny and resilient and the skin pliant and healthy. Begin bathing your Beagle at a young age, and he will grow to accept it (and even enjoy it!) as part of his grooming sessions when he's older.

Before bathing your Beagle, brush his coat thoroughly to remove any excess dirt and hair. The water in the bath should be lukewarm, not hot. Test the water temperature on the back of your hand before placing your dog in the tub. Purchase a dog shampoo from your local pet-supply store, which is specially formulated for a dog's coat. Human shampoos are made for human hair, not fur, and these products may dry out your Beagle's skin or burn his eyes. Be careful not to get shampoo or water in your dog's eyes and ears. Wash the head last to ensure that no shampoo drips into his eyes while you're bathing his body. Use a wet washcloth to sponge bathe your Beagle's face so as not to irritate his eyes and nose. Don't just bathe the top of the dog—reach under him and shampoo his belly and underparts so that no area is neglected. Rinsing the coat is just as important as soaping it. Thoroughly rinse the Beagle's coat until the water runs clear. Soap residue in the coat is worse than dirt, and it will dry out and irritate your dog's skin.

Lift your squeaky-clean Beagle from the bathtub and wrap him in a warm, clean towel. Hold the dog in your lap and assure him that he's prettier than ever—bonding with your Beagle is really what it's all about. Use towels to dry him as best as you can or use a blow-dryer set on low, avoiding his face. Keep him away from drafts and don't let him outside until he's completely dry. Make grooming a pleasant experience for your dog, and it will get easier every time.

THOSE FLOPPY EARS

Don't forget your Beagle's ears when grooming. Check inside the ear canals for any waxy buildup or unpleasant odor. If your Beagle is habitually scratching at his ears or if you see a thick brown discharge, he may have ear mites or an infection of some kind. A dog's ear canal is L-shaped, which makes infection more common than in human ears. Your veterinarian can recommend an ear-cleaning solution from the pet store. Use a dropper or a piece of cotton to flush the ear with the solution. The dog's immediate reaction will be to shake his head to get the water out of his ears—back up and let him shake. This will loosen the dirt and waxy buildup in his ears and make it easier for you to clean them out. Wipe the ear with a wadded tissue or cotton ball. Do not probe the ears with cotton swabs, as this could seriously damage your dog's ear or make an infection worse. Trim

Beagle Grooming Shopping List

Your Beagle is a wash-and-wear hound that requires little in the way of grooming. However, as a surprisingly heavy shedder, he does require weekly brushing and monthly bathing to keep his coat clean and healthy. Here are the basic items and products you will need to groom your Beagle:

BATHING

☐ Handheld spray attachment for your tub or sink

☐ Rubber mat for the dog to stand on

☐ Tearless dog shampoo and conditioner (don't use human products)

☐ Towels (a chamois is best)

☐ Pet hair dryer (you can use your own, but set it on low)

☐ Spritz-on dry shampoo (handy in case you need a quick cleanup to get rid of dirt or odor)

BRUSHING COAT

☐ Stainless steel comb

☐ Shedding blade or slicker brush

☐ Medium-length bristle brush or rubber curry comb

☐ Grooming mitt or hound glove

TRIMMING NAILS

☐ Dog nail cutters (scissor- or guillotine-type)

☐ Nail file or grinder

☐ Styptic pencil or styptic powder (in case you cut the quick)

BRUSHING TEETH

☐ Dog toothbrush or rough washcloth

☐ Dog toothpaste (don't use human toothpaste)

CLEANING EARS

☐ Cotton balls or wipes

☐ Liquid ear-cleaning solution

WIPING EYES

☐ Dog eye wipes

☐ Cotton balls

Shedding Season

Beagles shed a little coat every day, but for a few weeks twice a year—in the spring and fall—they drop lots of hair. During these heavy shedding periods, brush your Beagle's coat twice a day, morning and evening. A shedding blade will efficiently remove dead hair and keep the shedding seasons to a minimum. You'll be amazed at how much hair you will collect from your dog's coat! Use the blade gently against the Beagle's sensitive skin, and if you're using a regular brush, alternate brushing with and against the direction of hair growth for maximum hair removal.

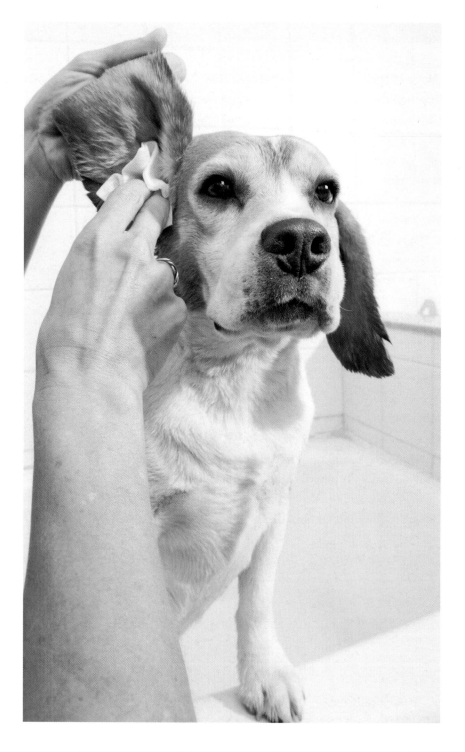

any excess hair growing around the ear vents to allow air to circulate. Fold the ears back until the canals are thoroughly dry. If you notice that there is something stuck in the ear, such as a large chunk of wax or a foreign object of some kind, don't try to remove it yourself. Take your Beagle to the vet and let a professional remove it. Your veterinarian has special training and special tools to help remove the item without damaging your Beagle's ear.

THOSE SOULFUL EYES

If you notice any redness or discharge in or around your Beagle's eye, he may have an injury or an infection of some kind. Caused by bacteria, conjunctivitis occurs commonly in dogs and can be treated with antibiotics from your veterinarian. Other possible causes for redness or discomfort may be a foreign object or excessive dust in the eye or a scratch from the family cat. Beagles live close to the floor, so keep your floors clean and dust free. Remember, Beagles like to chase real bunnies, not dust bunnies! It's always good to have an eye wash at home in case you need to quickly rinse out your Beagle's eyes in an emergency.

PEDICURE, ANYONE?

Most dogs are sensitive about having their feet touched, trimmed, or cleaned. As soon as your puppy comes home, begin massaging his feet. While he's sitting on your lap, hold a paw in your hand, massage his toes and footpads, and tell him how pretty his feet are. Handling your dog's feet regularly will make nail care and trimming so much easier. There's nothing worse than wrestling with your dog to give him a pedicure.

Examine your Beagle's feet at least once a week during your normal grooming sessions. Inspect his footpads to be sure that they are not cracked and that nothing is wedged or embedded between them. Walking the dog on pavement or blacktop will help wear down the nails, but not enough to avoid nail clipping entirely. Long nails can cause the toes to separate (or splay) and can be very uncomfortable for the dog. As such, you'll need to trim your dog's nails at least once or twice a month.

When bathing your Beagle, avoid soaping his face and eyes. Instead, use a washcloth to sponge these sensitive areas clean. Rinse him thoroughly with the help of a hand-held spray nozzle.

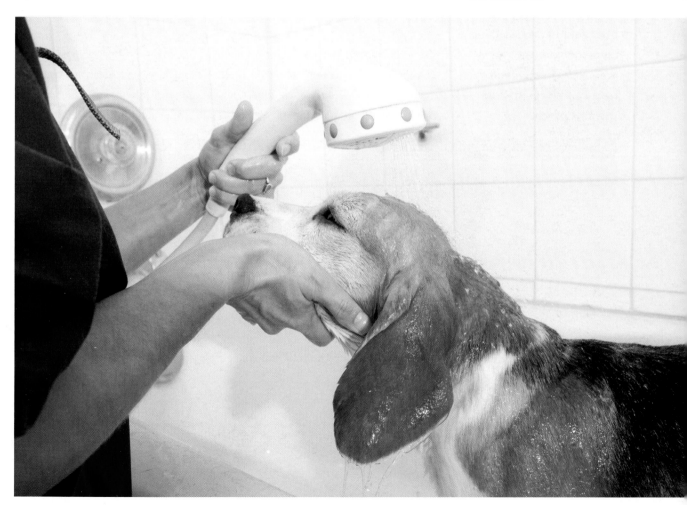

There are two different styles of nail-clipper: scissor- or guillotine-type. Do not use a human nail-clipper, as it may damage or splinter your dog's tough nails. Despite its name, the guillotine-type nail clipper is the kindest and gentlest. Don't be fooled by your puppy's crocodile tears: cutting his nails doesn't hurt. The best time to clip his nails is right after bathing, when the nails are soft from soaking in the tub. Light colored nails are easiest to trim because you can see the quick (the pink vein running through the nail). Avoid cutting the quick, which will hurt your pup. Have a styptic pencil or powder on hand in case you cause the nail to bleed. If your puppy has dark-colored nails, cutting only a little bit of the nail at a time is the safest approach.

Some Beagle owners prefer to use a grinder, which is faster and less stressful for both parties. If you're going to try this route, introduce the grinder to the puppy at a young age. Turn it on, set it on a nearby table, and give your puppy a treat. Ignore the sound of the grinder as you brush the puppy's coat. Once he is used to the sound, touch the side of the grinder to your dog's feet so that he gets used to the vibrating sensation. Some dogs are afraid of the buzzing sound and dislike the vibrating sensation on their feet. When it's time to actually use the grinder on the pup's nails, he will be accustomed to the noise and the feeling. The advantage of using the grinder is that you can't cut into the quick as easily, and if you do, the heat will instantly cauterize the bleeding. Nail grinders are sold online and in most pet-supply stores.

THOSE PEARLY WHITES

For a chowhound like the Beagle, his teeth are one of his most prized possessions. It's up to you to make sure that your Beagle's toothy grin stays clean and healthy throughout his life. Just like humans, dogs need their teeth brushed regularly to keep plaque and tartar buildup to a minimum. Neglecting your dog's teeth will

lead to bad breath, cavities, gum disease, loose or lost teeth, and possibly even liver, kidney, or heart disease.

Keep your Beagle's pearly whites healthy by brushing his teeth at least once a week. Use a dog toothbrush and dog toothpaste, both of which can be purchased at your local pet-supply store. (Don't use human toothpaste—its ingredients will make your dog sick.) Put a little bit of toothpaste on the brush at a time and lightly brush the outsides of your dog's teeth and along the gumline. You can also support good dental health by feeding your dog dry dog food and letting him chew on raw vegetables or hard bones that will scrape the excess plaque from his teeth.

GROOMING IMPORTANCE

Getting into a weekly grooming habit with your Beagle will do more than just keep him clean and happy. During your brushing, keep an eye out for any bumps, lumps, or bruises that may appear. If you notice anything strange that wasn't there the week before, such as a bump or evidence of parasites, take your Beagle to the veterinarian to get him checked out. Preventive health care is the best way to keep your Beagle healthy and thriving throughout his life—and thorough, habitual grooming is an easy way to keep an eye on your Beagle's health.

At a Glance ...

Desensitize your puppy to grooming at a young age. While you are relaxing on the couch or playing with your pup, feel all over his body—his face, belly, ears, mouth, and feet—so that he is familiar with your touch. This will make grooming a snap!

. . . .

Brush your Beagle weekly, and bathe him as needed. If your Beagle is outside for much of the day digging and working in the grass, he may need a bath more often than a suburban pup that spends most of his time indoors.

. . . .

During your weekly grooming sessions, be on the lookout for any changes in your Beagle's body from week to week. If you notice any bumps, lumps, or rashes, take your dog to the vet right away to be examined.

CHAPTER TEN

Healthy and Happy

Beagles are vigorous, active hounds blessed with long lives and overall good health. Providing your dog with a nutritious diet, a regular exercise routine, and annual veterinary visits for vaccinations and preventive health care are all that's required to keep a Beagle in the best of health. As a responsible owner, expect to do no less for your ever-loving, four-legged family member! You will be rewarded with a healthy, happy Beagle for the entirety of his life.

Find a veterinarian whom you will continue to use throughout your Beagle's life. As your Beagle ages, your vet will know his medical history firsthand and be better able to care for him.

VISITING THE VET

Some dogs don't mind going to the vet at all; others simply hate it and know exactly where they are as soon as they get out of the car. However, the Beagle is a friendly little fellow, so try to make his veterinary visits as fun and lighthearted as possible. If you feel apprehensive about the visit, your dog will too. Stay positive, and encourage your puppy with lots of praise and affection. Make going to the vet a fun experience, not a somber, scary one.

Finding the right veterinarian can be challenging. There may be too many practices in your area to choose from or not enough. Indeed, too many choices sometimes can be worse than too few. Ask your dog-owning friends for recommendations. Ideally, you want a vet whose practice is within easy driving distance. Ten miles is the farthest distance you should consider because it's important that you're able to get to the veterinarian's office quickly in an emergency. If you live in a rural area, check that the vet has plenty of experience with small companion animals (and not just livestock).

When searching for a veterinarian for your Beagle, here are a few questions to keep in mind:

1. How close is the office to your home? The office should be no more than fifteen minutes away in case of an emergency.

2. Does the vet have experience with Beagles (or small dogs, in general)?

3. Is the veterinarian and the clinic certified? Your state's veterinary medical board and the American Animal Hospital Association (AAHA) can verify certification. Visit www.aahanet.org for more information on veterinary certification.

4. Is the vet easy to talk to? The vet should make you feel like he or she has time for you and your dog and that he or she cares about your Beagle's well-being.

5. Does the practice offer the kind of health care you're interested in? If you're interested in a vet with an integrative approach, combining elements of conventional and holistic medicine, you'll have to look a bit harder.

6. What's the facility like? It is clean? Is the staff friendly and attentive? How long does it take to make an appointment? Is there parking? Is it bustling with happy clients and their pets?

7. Can you pay with a credit card? Are the fees for services explained clearly? How is billing done?

8. Can you board your dog there? Do they offer emergency and microchipping services?

Any relationship is a two-way street, and this includes your relationship with your veterinarian. Being courteous and respectful to your vet and his or her staff is a great place to start, even after you've waited for an hour and a half in the waiting room. Improve your rapport with your veterinarian by following these simple policies, which your vet will appreciate:

1. Be punctual to your appointment, and be patient while you're in the waiting room. It's very difficult for the veterinary staff to determine how long each pet will require in the examination room.

2. Teach your dog basic manners, including how to stand for examination. The vet's diagnosis will be easier and more accurate when handling a calm and obedient dog rather than a squirming, fearful one.

3. Always transport your Beagle in his crate or on a secure leash.

4. Make a list of questions for the vet and listen carefully to his or her answers. Follow his or her advice and take notes while you're in the exam room.

5. Don't skip appointments. Once his vaccinations are complete, your adult Beagle should see the vet at least once a year.

6. Pay attention to your dog's signs of good health, including his regular behavior at home, so that you can report changes to the vet.

A PIECE OF HISTORY

The original stock of Beagles in America derived from imports from British hunting kennels. Most likely due to crosses with Dachshunds, early American Beagles had crooked forelegs and were called "bench-legged." At the end of the nineteenth century, Beagles in the show rings were rangier and varied greatly in size, and hunting dogs showed more Dachshund and terrier tendencies. To refine the head, body, and running gear of the breed, James Kernochan began importing fine dogs from England and used them to set the desired hound type of today's Beagle.

7. Call the vet with questions before making an appointment. You can save time and money by not going to the vet for unnecessary visits.

8. In case of an emergency, phone the vet's office on the way so that they are ready for your arrival. Be sure you have the number saved in your cell phone.

VACCINATIONS

Breeders should make sure that puppies receive their first vaccinations at around five or six weeks of age. Upon purchasing the puppy, the breeder will give you a record of shots the puppy has received, when the booster shots are due, and which vaccinations your puppy still needs to get. Until your puppy is fully vaccinated, be sure to limit his contact with other dogs. Don't let this keep you from socializing your pup, but be sure that all dogs he comes in contact with have been fully vaccinated.

Schedule your puppy's first veterinarian exam within a few days of bringing him home. At the first visit, the vet will give the puppy a thorough exam to make sure that he's in good overall health, including a check of his heart, lungs, coat, mouth, and general condition. The vet will check the puppy's ears for mites, which are common in young pups. Take along a stool sample so the vet can check for internal parasites such as roundworms or hookworms. Though breeders should always deworm puppies prior to sale, it can sometimes be difficult to rid a puppy of internal parasites. It's best to have him double-checked at his first veterinary visit just to be sure he is worm free.

Your vet will also look at your puppy's health records from the breeder and discuss a schedule of vaccinations with you for your pup. Initial vaccines are usually given until the pup is about sixteen weeks old, after which the dog only

CORE Vaccines
Check with your vet, but all puppies should receive vaccines for the following diseases:

CONDITION	TREATMENT	PROGNOSIS	VACCINE NEEDED
ADENOVIRUS-2 (immunizes against Adenovirus-1, the agent of infectious canine hepatitis)	No curative therapy for infectious hepatitis; treatment geared toward minimizing neurologic effects, shock, hemorrhage, secondary infections	Self-limiting but cross-protects against infectious hepatitis, which is highly contagious and can be mild to rapidly fatal	Recommended
DISTEMPER	No specific treatment; supportive treatment (IV fluids, antibiotics)	High mortality rates	Highly recommended
PARVOVIRUS-2	No specific treatment; supportive treatment (IV fluids, antibiotics)	Highly contagious to young puppies; high mortality rates	Highly recommended
RABIES	No treatment	Fatal	Required

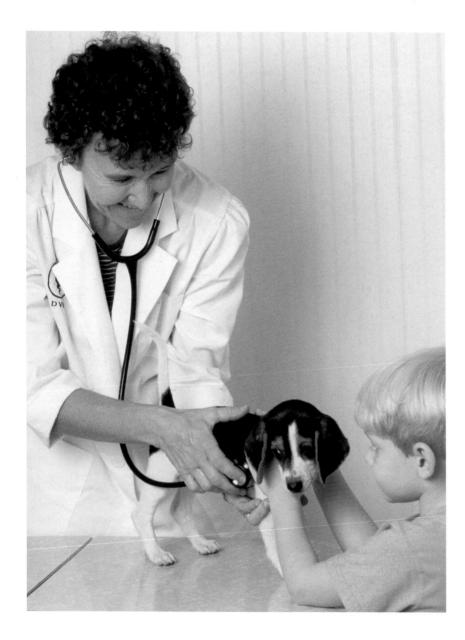

Spaying and Neutering

What was once the great debate for dog owners has become a no-brainer. If you're not going to show or breed your Beagle, you should spay or neuter your dog. The American Kennel Club believes that this is the most responsible choice for pet owners, and there are many benefits for choosing this option. The surgical procedures for spaying a female dog and neutering a male dog are routine surgeries for most experienced veterinarians. While there is risk with any kind of surgery, spaying and neutering are not considered dangerous and dogs fully recover within a few days to a week. Statistics show that spayed females are less likely to develop uterine infections and mammary cancer, and neutered males have a lower risk of developing prostate and testicular cancer.

needs annual boosters. Discuss with your vet which vaccinations he or she feels are required. This will depend on where you live and how frequently your dog encounters other dogs.

The American Veterinary Medical Association (AVMA) recommends a series of "core" vaccines that all dogs should receive no matter where in the country they live. These core vaccinations protect your Beagle against the most serious diseases that affect dogs in the United States. Core vaccinations include canine distemper (CDV), canine parvovirus (CPV), canine adenovirus (CAV2), and canine hepatitis (CA1). Rabies immunization is required in all fifty states, with the vaccine given three weeks after the complete series of puppy shots.

"Noncore" vaccines are those recommended by the AVMA when the risk is present. As such, there are different vaccination requirements for different regions of the country. A few common noncore vaccines are canine parainfluenza, leptospirosis, coronavirus, Bordetella (kennel cough) and Lyme disease (borreliosis). Your veterinarian will advise you about which of these affect your dog most depending on where you live and on your Beagle's lifestyle.

Thin Is In

We've discussed the importance of keeping your Beagle trim by portioning out his daily food and limiting treats and table scraps. While it can be embarrassing and upsetting to hear your friends joking about your roly-poly Beagle, it's really more than your ego at stake. The dog's health can eventually deteriorate from the added pounds on his small frame. Common side effects of obesity in Beagles include orthopedic problems like arthritis and vertebral deterioration, and torn tendons and ligaments, as well as heart disease, respiratory problems, diabetes, immune disorders, and skin conditions.

The AVMA has a helpful webpage describing the common pet vaccinations at www.avma.org/public/PetCare/Pages/vaccinations.aspx. For a more detailed report on common core and noncore vaccinations recommended for your puppy, visit the American Animal Hospital Association's website at www.aahanet.org /Library/CanineVaccine.aspx.

KNOW YOUR ENEMY

All breeds can suffer from hereditary or genetic disorders, and the National Beagle Club of America lists the following conditions as notable in the breed: seizure disorders, hypothyroidism, allergies, hip dysplasia, and intervertebral disk disease. Don't hesitate to ask your breeder about these conditions when you are looking for a puppy. Not all disorders can be tested, but a responsible breeder will acknowledge these common disorders in the breed and reassure you of the health of their puppies and dogs. Breeders should have health screening certificates and health guarantees for all of their breeding stock to prove that they have tested for possible genetic disorders and that their dogs are hearty and healthy.

Visit the NBC's website, http://clubs.akc.org/NBC, for more information about these and other conditions that owners should be on the lookout for:

Seizure disorders: Epilepsy is a brain dysfunction that manifests itself through seizures of varying severity, from mild twitching to extreme convulsions or fits. Epilepsy is an evasive disease, or rather, a set of symptoms occurring seemingly without cause, described as "lightning in the brain," an electrical storm due to physical and chemical conditions in the brain, which misfires signals to the body. The causes of epilepsy are various and often unknown (referred to as idiopathic); epilepsy can be genetic or acquired through infection, trauma, tumors, or toxins. While the general onset of epilepsy is between eighteen and twenty-four months old, Beagles can begin showing signs at any age, with stress the likely trigger. Whether genetic or acquired, epilepsy can be managed in Beagles, usually without the use of anticonvulsant drugs. Discuss any noticeable changes in your dog's behavior with your veterinarian.

Other Vaccines and Treatment

Depending on where you live and your dog's needs, the following ailments and diseases can be treated through your veterinarian:

CONDITION	TREATMENT	PROGNOSIS	RECOMMENDATION
BORDETELLA (KENNEL COUGH)	Keep warm; humidify room; moderate exercise	Highly contagious; rarely fatal in healthy dogs; easily treated	Optional vaccine; prevalence varies; vaccine may be linked to acute reactions; low efficacy
FLEA AND TICK INFESTATION	Topical and ingestible	Highly contagious	Preventive treatment highly recommended
HEARTWORM	Arsenical compound; rest; restricted exercise	Widely occurring infections; preventive programs available regionally; successful treatment after early detection	Preventive treatment highly recommended
INTESTINAL WORMS	Dewormer; home medication regimen	Good with prompt treatment	Preventive treatment highly recommended
LYME DISEASE (BORRELIOSIS)	Antibiotics	Can't completely eliminate the organism, but can be controlled in most cases	Vaccine recommended only for dogs with high risk of exposure to deer ticks
PARAINFLUENZA	Rest; humidify room; moderate exercise	Highly contagious; mild; self-limiting; rarely fatal	Vaccine optional but recommended; doesn't block infection, but lessens clinical signs
PERIODONTITIS	Dental cleaning; extractions; repair	Excellent, but involves anesthesia	Preventive treatment recommended

Hypothyroidism: Hypothyroidism occurs when the thyroid gland is no longer able to produce sufficient hormones to sustain normal good health. Because the disease is genetic, breeders are encouraged to screen all dogs once they reach puberty. Treatment to correct the thyroid imbalance with a thyroid supplement (given twice daily) is routinely advised by veterinarians.

Allergies: Allergies affect most two-legged and four-legged mammals on the planet. It's estimated that one in five dogs exhibits some kind of allergic condition. Signs of allergies vary greatly and are frequently missed or misdiagnosed. Itching, loss of coat, ear inflammation, eye tearing, vomiting, coughing, and trouble breathing can all be signs of allergies. Just like humans, dogs can be

Support Canine Health Research

AMERICAN KENNEL CLUB

The mission of the American Kennel Club Canine Health Foundation, Inc. (AKC CHF) is to advance the health of all dogs by funding sound scientific research and supporting the dissemination of health information to prevent, treat, and cure canine disease. The foundation makes grants to fund a variety of health efforts:

- Identifying the cause(s) of disease
- Earlier, more accurate diagnosis
- Developing screening tests for breeders
- Accurate, positive prognosis
- Effective, efficient treatment

The AKC CHF also supports educational programs that bring scientists together to discuss their work and develop new collaborations to further advance canine health.

The AKC created the foundation in 1995 to raise funds to support canine health research. Each year the AKC CHF allocates $1.5 million to new health-research projects.

How You Can Help: If you have an AKC-registered dog, submit his DNA sample (cheek swab or blood sample) to the Canine Health Information Center (CHIC) DNA databank (www.caninehealthinfo.org). Encourage regular health testing by breeders, get involved with your local dog club, and support the efforts to host health-education programs. And, if possible, make a donation.

For information, contact the AKC Canine Health Foundation, P.O. Box 900061, Raleigh, NC 27675-9061 or check out the website at www.akcchf.org.

allergic to grass, fleas, food, plastic, shampoo, dust, cigarette smoke, and many other ordinary, common things in their environment. If your Beagle is constantly chewing at his feet and coat or showing other signs of discomfort, you should discuss this with your vet. Food allergies are particularly challenging because you have to identify the ingredient (or ingredients) that is causing the reaction.

Hip dysplasia: A common orthopedic problem in purebred dogs, hip dysplasia is the poor development of the hip joint, causing arthritis and possibly lameness in the dog. Usually associated with large breeds like the German Shepherd Dog and Rottweiler, hip dysplasia can affect small dogs like the Beagle as well. Hip dysplasia is caused by genetic as well as environmental factors. Breeders are encouraged to have their Beagles' hips screened and submit the results to the Orthopedic Foundation for Animals (www.offa.org).

Intervertebral disk disease (IVDD): The Beagle, like the Dachshund and Pekingese, are predisposed to IVDD due to their normal-sized bodies with short legs. IVDD usually affects the neck vertebrae in Beagles around three years of age and older. The intervertebral disks are the cushions between the vertebrae that make the spine flexible. IVDD causes the disks to dry out and lose their flexibility, eventually protruding from the spine and possibly rupturing. Affected dogs experience neck and back pain and become reluctant to take stairs or jump up on furniture. Severe cases require a surgical procedure called disk fenestration, though steroids and strict crate rest can alleviate pain in mild cases. Physical therapy is recommended for dogs that have lost the ability to walk.

CHECKING FOR PARASITES

While brushing your dog's coat, be on the lookout for signs of parasites: small black specs in your dog's coat, red irritated skin, a rash, or the actual insects themselves. If your Beagle is biting at his coat or scratching himself excessively,

Ten Signs of a Healthy Beagle

The more time you spend with your Beagle, the better you will know him. Recognizing the signs of normal good health and behavior—and taking note of any changes—will ensure that you know when it's time to visit the vet. Here are ten signs that your Beagle is healthy and happy:

1. Clear, bright, shiny eyes
2. Shiny, smooth, and resilient coat without any red areas, flakes, or scabs
3. A moist, cool nose
4. Good appetite and activity level
5. Firm stool with no blood or other discharge
6. Clean smelling breath and ears
7. Normal thirst and urination
8. Light pink, clean ears with little wax buildup
9. Pink, firm gums and white teeth
10. A trim outline, with a visible tuckup under his belly

Not all puppies receive the same vaccinations. Discuss the mandatory and recommended vaccines for your area with your veterinarian and breeder.

it's a major clue that your dog may have an infestation of some kind. External parasites—namely fleas, ticks, and mites—can be very uncomfortable for the dog and lead to skin and coat conditions. Use a flea comb (a metal comb with thin, close teeth) to go through the coat. Wipe the comb clean with a paper towel after each stroke and look for black specks.

Fleas are a nuisance, but they are relatively easy to deal with. If you suspect your dog has fleas, ask your veterinarian for a preventive flea remedy. Flea remedies usually come in either liquid or pill form, which you will give your dog on a monthly basis. Though this will take care of your dog's flea problem on his body, you also must address the resultant flea problem in your home. When there are fleas on a dog, there will be fleas in the home—in his bed, on the couch, in the carpet, and in the backyard. You will have to vacuum the house thoroughly and then spray or "bomb" the house with an insecticide formulated to kill adult fleas and the immature forms of eggs, larvae, and pupae.

Ticks are easier to spot than fleas—they're larger, for one. Look around the dog's neck, on his stomach, under his legs, and in his ears. If you do spot a tick, use a pair of tweezers to remove the insect carefully. Watch the site over the next few days to be sure that it doesn't become inflamed. Ticks can carry an assortment of diseases such as Lyme disease (borreliosis), Rocky Mountain spotted fever, Colorado tick fever, and ehrlichiosis. If you live in a tick-prone area, your veterinarian will most likely suggest a few extra vaccinations to protect your dog against these diseases.

In addition to fleas and ticks, always be on the lookout for ear mites. Ear mites are too small for the human eye to see, but a brown discharge with some odor in the ear is a clear indication that they are present. Your vet will confirm with a microscope that ear mites are the case, and he or she will prescribe you a preparation to remedy the problem.

A host of intestinal worms can also infest your dog, and these internal parasites are even more serious than fleas and ticks. The most common worms, roundworms (ascarids) are usually contracted by puppies from their mothers and littermates, but they can also be contracted from rodents or from contaminated water or food sources. Other internal parasites include hookworms, whipworms, and tapeworms, all of which can be identified in the dog's feces. If you suspect your dog may have intestinal worms, bring a stool sample to your veterinarian. He or she will assess the sample for any worm segments or larvae.

Heartworms are the most dreaded parasites, but they are also the most preventable. Heartworms are transmitted by mosquitoes and can cause heart disease in dogs. Symptoms of heartworm infestation (or any intestinal worm infestation for that matter) include a distended belly, vomiting, diarrhea, trouble going to the bathroom, dry hair, and weight loss. Your veterinarian will recommend a monthly oral preventive based on your Beagle's age and lifestyle. Routine worming is essential throughout a dog's life and a suitable preventive regimen prescribed by a veterinarian is advised.

THE GOLDEN BEAGLE

As your Beagle ages, you'll need to keep a closer eye on him to make sure he remains healthy and happy from day to day. Once your Beagle is eight years old, start taking him to the veterinarian for twice-yearly checkups. Preventive care is the best health care you can afford for senior dogs. Make his life a little easier by feeding him a specially formulated diet for senior dogs, shortening your daily walks, and providing ramps and steps around the house. Your Beagle will be thankful for these little things that make his life easier and more comfortable. With good nutrition, routine grooming, and dedicated health care, your Beagle will remain spry and energetic throughout his golden years.

At a Glance ...

Finding the right veterinarian is no easy task. Ask for recommendations from your breeder and other dog owners who live nearby. Choose a veterinarian who is no farther than fifteen minutes from your home and whom you are comfortable with.

Your veterinarian will help you decide on which vaccinations are best for your Beagle based on where you live and on your dog's lifestyle. Visit the American Veterinary Medical Association (AVMA) website at www.avma.org/issues/vaccination for more information on the recommended vaccines for your region.

Be on the lookout for common parasites such as fleas, ticks, and ear mites on your Beagle. Your veterinarian may prescribe a monthly remedy to prevent an assortment of external and internal parasites in your Beagle.

Beagles on the Move

Beagles are busy little dogs that like to keep moving! The best way to keep your Beagle happy is to involve him in your family outings, weekend errands, and fun excursions. How active your Beagle is will depend entirely on your own schedule and lifestyle. Your dog will not be satisfied watching you catch up on the latest season of *True Blood* or surf eBay for doggy collectibles. A Beagle's idea of fun includes fresh air, soft grass, and critters to chase! Exercise is

not optional when it comes to a Beagle. A good morning walk or jog will clear his head and keep him focused for hours. An underexercised Beagle is quickly bored with his routine and will be unhappy left at home.

Investigating the world with all its glorious smells and sights will keep your Beagle's senses keen and his mind alert. It will also keep him fit, which is critical for a breed that loves suppertime as much as the Beagle does. Keep him in the peak of physical condition for as many years as possible. A sedentary lifestyle for a Beagle is a recipe for obesity, boredom, and bad behavior.

As tempting as it may be to allow your Beagle off leash at the park or beach, don't do it. Even the best trained Beagles are not 100 percent reliable off leash. First and foremost, your Beagle is a scenthound and his hunting instinct will trump any training. He will follow his nose wherever it takes him, especially toward that alluring smell on the other side of the fence, across the street, or down the block.

If you are interested in getting involved in more formal activities, the American Kennel Club hosts thousands of events each year for owners and their dogs, including dog shows, agility trials, field trials, obedience trails, Rally, and tracking. The first step toward getting involved in these AKC events is to join a dog-training club or a local Beagle breed club. You can visit the AKC website (www.akc.org) or the National Beagle Club of America website (http://clubs.akc .org/NBC) for a listing of clubs in your area.

Interested in taking basic obedience to the next level? Beagles are natural athletes, commonly competing in high-energy sports such as Rally and agility.

CONFORMATION

Conformation is the formal name for dog shows, in which judges select their winning dogs based on how closely they conform to the breed standard. Dog shows are essentially elimination contests, as the best Beagles in each class compete to determine one winner for 13-inch and one winner for 15-inch Beagles. Those two Best of Variety winners compete in the Hound Group, and then the winner of each Group competes for Best in Show. At the end of the day, only one dog remains undefeated over possibly thousands of others.

Beginners can enter match competitions hosted by local dog clubs, which are more informal than dog shows and give newcomers experience showing their dogs. If you are interested in showing your Beagle, be sure to let your breeder know this when you are searching for a puppy. A show-quality Beagle will be more expensive than a pet-quality pup, but your breeder will help you choose a puppy with all of the right physical and behavioral qualities of a prospective show dog. Search the AKC website, www.akc.org, or the National Beagle Club of America website, http://clubs.akc.org/NBC, for information about local dog shows near you, and visit a few shows to see what show competition is like. The Beagle breeders at the show will be happy to talk with you about the sport and give you some advice on how to get involved.

Few people ever think to attend a dog show as a fun weekend outing. If you love dogs, dog shows are great family fun. Dog shows sponsored by the American Kennel Club are actually not very difficult to find, especially because there are about four thousand shows held annually. Dog shows vary in size from the large all-breed shows that you may see on television, such as the Westminster Kennel Club dog show in February or the AKC Eukanuba National Championship in December, to smaller shows that may only attract a few hundred dogs. There are also specialty shows, which are for a single breed or Group. For Beagle enthusiasts, attending the National Beagle Club's national specialty show is the perfect way to see Beagles in action. This all-Beagle show includes a puppy sweepstakes, regular conformation classes, Junior Showmanship, obedience, Rally, agility, and tracking. You can find information on the show at www.nbcspecialty.com.

OBEDIENCE AND RALLY

In the AKC sport of obedience, dog and handler teams are judged on how precisely they execute a particular exercise, such as heeling, standing for examination, a long jump, or a directed retrieve. There are three levels of obedience, each one increasing in difficulty: Novice Class, Open Class, and Utility Class. The Novice Class focuses on companion skills, such as heeling (both with and without a leash), figure eights, coming when called, standing for examination, and staying in both a sit (for one minute) and a down position (for three minutes) with a group of dogs. After receiving three qualifying scores under two different judges, dogs can earn the Companion Dog (CD) title. In the Open Class, dogs must work off leash, and jumping and retrieving exercises are added. The Companion Dog Excellent (CDX) title is awarded at this level. In the most difficult level, the Utility Class, dogs must perform scent discrimination, directed retrieves, jumping exercises, and silent signal cues. The Utility Dog (UD) title is awarded at this class. Beyond the UD title, dogs can earn the Utility Dog Excellent (UDX) and the Obedience Trial Champion (OTCH), the highest award an obedience dog can earn. Visit www.akc.org/events/obedience for more information on obedience and how to get involved.

AKC Rally is a much newer sport and requires that a dog and handler work together using similar skills to those needed in obedience. Modeled after rally-style auto racing, Rally allows teams to move at their own pace, progressing through ten to twenty stations, each with a different sign indicating an exercise to perform. There are three levels: Novice, Advanced, and Excellent, with the complexity and difficulty increasing at each level. For more information on AKC Rally, visit www.akc.org/events/rally.

AGILITY TRIALS

The AKC held its first agility trial in 1994. Although a fledgling compared to obedience, agility has gained tremendous popularity in the past decade. A fun-filled obstacle course for dog and handler, agility is as much fun to watch as it is to compete! The Standard Class features obstacles such as the seesaw, dog walk, and A-frame as well as a variety of jumps, weave poles, tunnels, and pause tables. Teams are judged on speed, accuracy, timing, and distance handling. In addition to the Standard Class, there are Jumpers with Weaves, Fifteen and Send Time (FAST), and Preferred Classes, each with different obstacles and regulations. There are three levels of competition, varying in levels of difficulty: Novice, Open, and Excellent. The AKC website (www.akc.org) includes details about each level, requirements, scoring, titles, and more. The highest title achieved in agility is the Master Agility Champion (MACH).

Agility can be difficult for beginners due to the large obstacles and equipment needed to train for the sport. Contact your local Beagle breed club for information on how to begin training your dog for agility. Many breed clubs or local agility organizations have fields and equipment that you can practice on with your dog. Visit the AKC website, www.akc.org/events/agility, for more information on the sport, and contact the National Beagle Club of America, http://clubs.akc.org/NBC, to find a local Beagle club near you.

TRACKING

Tracking is a nose sport, a favorite among the breeds of the Hound Group! A dog is judged on how well he demonstrates his natural ability to recognize and follow a scent left on an article of clothing (usually a leather glove). The dog follows the scent of the article through a specified area. Tracking is the basis of canine disciplines such as search and rescue, drug and arson detection, police work, and USDA search work. It's not just the mighty Bloodhound that excels in finding missing persons or the St. Bernard that saves a child in an avalanche. All dogs can scent and track, though scenthounds (like your Beagle) have the natural advantages of their broad nostrils, large ears, and long muzzles. Some AKC clubs offer tracking classes—all you need is a harness, a 20- to 40-foot leash, and a dog with a nose that knows. Titles in tracking include Tracking Dog (TD), Tracking Dog Excellent (TDX), Variable Surface Tracking (VST), and Champion Tracker (CT). Find out more at www.akc.org/events/tracking.

BEAGLE FIELD TRIALS

Beagle clubs originally were established to promote and preserve the tracking and field instincts of the small scenthound. Unique to North America, Beagle field trials trace their origins to the 1890s when the first field trial event was hosted by a group of owners (a group that would eventually become the National Beagle Club of America, the breed's future parent club). At that time, Beagles competed in large packs to flush out rabbits from the field. Eighteen dogs attended the first trial, and within six years, three formal packs were registered with the new club.

In the early 1900s, as the Beagle's popularity began to soar, owners who couldn't afford to maintain a large pack began promoting the idea of hunting with only one or two Beagles at a time instead of a full pack. Beagles selectively bred to work independently to trail a rabbit or hare became known as "singles."

Today, the National Beagle Club offers four different types of field trial: Brace, for opposite-sex pairs in pursuit of a wild rabbit or hare; Gun Dog Brace, which includes a gun-shyness test; Small Pack, for four- to seven-hound packs in pursuit of a rabbit (Small Pack Option also includes a gun-shyness test); and Large Pack, held in the northern United States where snowshoe hare are plentiful, for hound packs of twenty or more. A fifth format, the Formal Pack, is a non-AKC hunting event made up of privately owned Beagles, often supported by additional Beagles owned by members from a local group.

Field trials and actual hunting are quite similar, though field-trial dogs work slower and more deliberately to follow a specific scent track. Dogs must be eager to pursue the quarry, identify the cover, and not be deterred by the conditions. Beagles voice their progress when hot on the trail and must follow the trail closely and efficiently. Always adaptable to changes in the environment, Beagles are persistent, patient, and untiring when working. Determination and independence are prized in the field, as is a strong sense of competition without dishonoring fellow pack members. Judges award points for all of these virtues during field-trial competition.

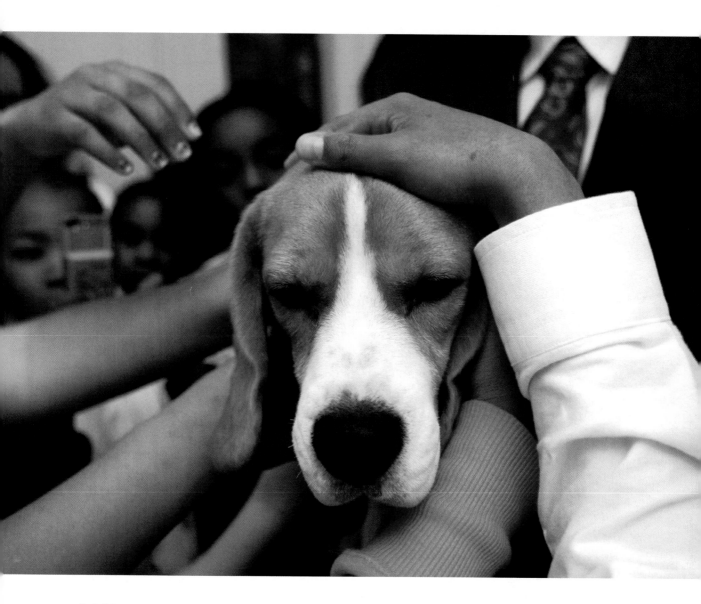

Beagle field trials may only be held in areas where the quarry is indigenous to the territory. Although rabbits are famous for their ability to multiply, it is very difficult to introduce rabbits and hares into a strange territory. Today, over 500 Beagle clubs either own or lease their own expanses of land with the desired food supply and cover to maintain a healthy population of rabbits. Beagle field trials remain the most popular type of trial in the country, with over 50,000 entrants (or starters) in over 700 trials annually. To learn more about field trials, visit the National Beagle Club of America's website, http://clubs.akc.org/NBC, or the AKC website, www.akc.org/events/field_trials/beagles.

Uno, the only Beagle to win Best in Show at the Westminster Kennel Club dog show, is a dedicated therapy dog to both children and adults. All dogs, no matter their pedigree or breed, have the potential to become therapy dogs.

THERAPY DOGS

Beagles make natural therapy dogs. Owners of well-trained, socialized Beagles can take advantage of their dog's affable personality and cute-as-a-button appearance by visiting nursing homes, care facilities, and hospitals to meet and greet those in need.

The ten skills included in the Canine Good Citizen test are required for all therapy dogs, and most registries require therapy dogs to have a CGC certification before visiting any hospitals or care facilities. Passing the Canine Good Citizen

The AKC Code of Sportsmanship

- Sportsmen respect the history, traditions, and integrity of the sport of purebred dogs.
- Sportsmen commit themselves to values of fair play, honesty, courtesy, and vigorous competition, as well as winning and losing with grace.
- Sportsmen refuse to compromise their commitment and obligation to the sport of purebred dogs by injecting personal advantage or consideration into their decisions or behavior.
- The sportsman judge judges only on the merits of the dogs and considers no other factors.
- The sportsman judge or exhibitor accepts constructive criticism.
- The sportsman exhibitor declines to enter or exhibit under a judge where it might reasonably appear that the judge's placements could be based on something other than the merits of the dogs.
- The sportsman exhibitor refuses to compromise the impartiality of a judge.
- The sportsman respects the American Kennel Club's bylaws, rules, regulations, and policies governing the sport of purebred dogs.
- Sportsmen find that vigorous competition and civility are not inconsistent and are able to appreciate the merit of their competition and the efforts of competitors.
- Sportsmen welcome, encourage, and support newcomers to the sport.
- Sportsmen will deal fairly with all those who trade with them.
- Sportsmen are willing to share honest and open appraisals of both the strengths and weaknesses of their breeding stock.
- Sportsmen spurn any opportunity to take personal advantage of positions offered or bestowed upon them.
- Sportsmen always consider as paramount the welfare of their dogs.
- Sportsmen refuse to embarrass the sport, the American Kennel Club, or themselves while taking part in the sport.

test is the first step toward becoming a therapy dog team. The second step is to register your dog with one of the many therapy dog organizations that work with owner-and-dog teams to match available dogs with therapy assignments at participating facilities.

The AKC currently works with over fifty-five organizations, including Pet Partners® (www.petpartners.org), Therapy Dogs Incorporated (www.therapydogs.com), Bright and Beautiful Therapy Dogs (www .golden-dogs.org), Therapy Dogs International (www.tdi-dog.org), and Love on a Leash (www.loveonaleash.org). The AKC Therapy Dog Program, introduced in 2011, awards the Therapy Dog (ThD) title to certified therapy dogs that perform fifty or more visits. For more information, visit www.akc .org/akctherapydog.

A FRIEND FOR LIFE

No matter how you stay active with your Beagle, whether it's through organized AKC activities, therapy work, daily jogs, or simply going to the dog park on the weekends, your Beagle will be overjoyed to spend time with you, his favorite person and best friend. Beagles are jovial, expressive little dogs with big hearts that love to bask in the limelight of their owner's affections. Stay active throughout your Beagle's life and you will be rewarded with a loyal friend for many years to come.

At a Glance ...

If your Beagle takes to basic obedience training with ease, get involved in one of the many organized AKC activities such as obedience, agility, Rally, or field trials. Regardless of whether you win or lose, you will have fun getting involved in the community and meeting other Beagle owners just like you.

There's no doubt that Beagles love people. Share your Beagle's affection with those in need by becoming a therapy dog-and-owner team. Your Beagle's soulful eyes and loving face may be just what the doctor ordered for those in need of a furry pick-me-up.

No matter whether they were bred for the home, the field, or the conformation ring, all Beagles enjoy vigorous activity and exercise with their favorite human—you! Keep your Beagle physically healthy and mentally active and you will be rewarded with a devoted companion throughout your Beagle's life.

Resources

BOOKS

The American Kennel Club's Meet the Breeds: Dog Breeds from A to Z, 2012 edition (Irvine, California: BowTie Press, 2011) The ideal puppy buyer's guide, this book has all you need to know about each breed currently recognized by the AKC.

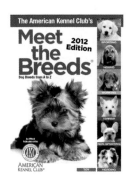

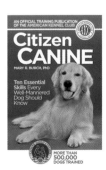

The Complete Dog Book, 20th edition (New York: Ballantine Books, 2006) This official publication of the AKC, first published in 1929, includes the complete histories and breed standards of 153 recognized breeds, as well as information on general care and the dog sport.

The Complete Dog Book for Kids (New York: Howell Book House, 1996) Specifically geared toward young people, this official publication of the AKC presents 149 breeds and varieties, as well as introductory owners' information.

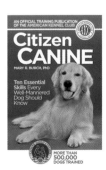

Citizen Canine: Ten Essential Skills Every Well-Mannered Dog Should Know by Mary R. Burch, PhD (Freehold, New Jersey: Kennel Club Books, 2010) This official AKC publication is the definitive guide to the AKC's Canine Good Citizen® Program, recognized as the gold standard of behavior for dogs, with more than half a million dogs trained.

DOGS: The First 125 Years of the American Kennel Club (Freehold, New Jersey: Kennel Club Books, 2009) This official AKC publication presents an authoritative, complete history of the AKC, including detailed information not found in any other volume.

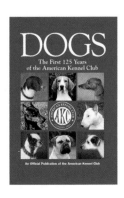

Dog Heroes of September 11th: A Tribute to America's Search and Rescue Dogs, 10th anniversary edition, by Nona Kilgore Bauer (Freehold, New Jersey: Kennel Club Books, 2011) A publication to salute the canines that served in the recovery missions following the September 11th attacks, this book serves as a lasting tribute to these noble American heroes.

The Original Dog Bible: The Definitive Source for All Things Dog, 2nd edition, by Kristin Mehus-Roe (Irvine, California: BowTie Press, 2009) This 831-page magnum opus includes more than 250 breed profiles, hundreds of color photographs, and a wealth of information on every dog topic imaginable—thousands of practical tips on grooming, training, care, and much more.

PERIODICALS

American Kennel Club Gazette

Every month since 1889, serious dog fanciers have looked to the *AKC Gazette* for authoritative advice on training, showing, breeding, and canine health. Each issue

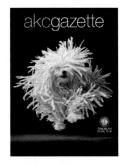

includes the breed columns section, written by experts from the respective breed clubs. Only available electronically.

AKC Family Dog

This is a bimonthly magazine for the dog lover whose special dog is "just a pet." Helpful tips, how-tos, and features are written in an entertaining and reader-friendly format. It's a lifestyle magazine for today's busy families who want to enjoy a rewarding, mutually happy relationship with their canine companions.

Dog Fancy

The world's most widely read dog magazine, *Dog Fancy* celebrates dogs and the people who love them. Each monthly issue includes info on cutting-edge medical developments, health and fitness (with a focus on prevention, treatment, and natural

therapy), behavior and training, travel and activities, breed profiles and dog news, issues and trends for purebred and mixed-breed dog owners. The magazine informs, inspires, and entertains while promoting responsible dog ownership. Throughout its more than forty-year history, *Dog Fancy* has garnered numerous honors, including being named the Best All-Breed Magazine by the Dog Writers Association of America.

Dogs in Review

For more than fifteen years, *Dogs in Review* has showcased the finest dogs in the United States and from around the world. The emphasis has always been on strong content, with input

from distinguished breeders, judges, and handlers worldwide. This global perspective distinguishes this monthly publication from its competitors—no other North American dog-show magazine gathers together so many international experts to enlighten and entertain its readership.

Dogs USA

Dogs USA is an annual lifestyle magazine published by the editors of *Dog Fancy* that covers all aspects of the dog world: culture, art, history, travel, sports, and science. It also profiles breeds to help prospective owners choose the best dogs for their future needs, such as a potential show champion, super service dog, great pet, or competitive star.

Natural Dog

Natural Dog is the magazine dedicated to giving a dog a natural lifestyle. From nutritional choices to grooming to dog-supply options, this publication helps readers make the transition from traditional to natural methods. The

magazine also explores the array of complementary treatments available for today's dogs: acupuncture,

massage, homeopathy, aromatherapy, and much more. *Natural Dog* appears as an annual publication and also as the flip side of *Dog Fancy* magazine four times a year (in February, May, August, and November).

Puppies USA

Also from the editors of *Dog Fancy,* this annual magazine offers essential information for all new puppy owners. *Puppies USA* is lively and informative, including advice on general care, nutrition, grooming, and training techniques for all puppies, whether purebred or mixed breed, adopted, rescued, or purchased. In addition, it offers family fun through quizzes, contests, and much more. An extensive breeder directory is included.

WEBSITES

www.akc.org

The American Kennel Club (AKC) website is an excellent starting point for researching dog breeds and learning about puppy care. The site lists hundreds of breeders, along with basic information about breed selection and basic care. The site also has links to the national breed club of every AKC-recognized breed; breed-club sites offer plenty of detailed breed information, as well as lists of member breeders. In addition, you can find the AKC National Breed Club Rescue List at www.akc.org/breeds/rescue.cfm. If looking for purebred puppies, go to www.puppybuyerinfo.com for AKC classifieds and parent-club referrals.

www.dogchannel.com

Powered by *Dog Fancy*, Dog Channel is "the website for dog lovers," where hundreds of thousands of visitors each month find extensive information on breeds, training, health and nutrition, puppies, care, activities, and more. Interactive features include forums, Dog College, games, and Club Dog, a free club where dog lovers can create blogs for their pets and earn points to buy products. Dog Channel is the one-stop site for all things dog.

www.meetthebreeds.com

The official website of the AKC Meet the Breeds® event, hosted by the American Kennel Club in the Jacob Javits Center in New York City in the fall. The first Meet the Breeds event took place in 2009. The website includes information on every recognized breed of dog and cat, alphabetically listed, as well as the breeders, demonstration facilitators, sponsors, and vendors participating in the annual event.

AKC AFFILIATES

The **AKC Museum of the Dog**, established in 1981, is located in St. Louis, Missouri, and houses the world's finest collection of art devoted to the dog. Visit www.museumofthedog.org.

The **AKC Humane Fund** promotes the joy and value of responsible and productive pet ownership through education, outreach, and grant-making. Monies raised may fund grants to organizations that teach responsible pet ownership; provide for the health and well-being of all dogs; and preserve and celebrate the human-animal bond and the evolutionary relationship between dogs and humankind. Go to www.akchumanefund.org.

The **American Kennel Club Companion Animal Recovery (CAR) Corporation** is dedicated to reuniting lost microchipped and tattooed pets with their owners. AKC CAR maintains a permanent-identification database and provides lifetime recovery services 24 hours a day, 365 days a year, for all animal species. Millions of pets are enrolled in the program, which was established in 1995. Visit www.akccar.org.

The **American Kennel Club Canine Health Foundation (AKC CHF), Inc.** is the largest foundation in the world to fund canine-only health studies for purebred and mixed-breed dogs. More than $22 million has been allocated in research funds to more than 500 health studies conducted to help dogs live longer, healthier lives. Go to www.akcchf.org.

AKC PROGRAMS

The **Canine Good Citizen Program (CGC)** was established in 1989 and is designed to recognize dogs that have good manners at home and in the community. This rapidly growing, nationally recognized program stresses responsible dog ownership for owners and basic training and good manners for dogs. All dogs that pass the ten-step Canine Good Citizen test receive a certificate from the American Kennel Club. Go to www.akc.org/events/cgc.

The **AKC S.T.A.R. Puppy Program** is designed to get dog owners and their puppies off to a good start and is aimed at loving dog owners who have taken the time to attend basic obedience classes with their puppies. After completing a six-week training course, the puppy must pass the AKC S.T.A.R. Puppy test, which evaluates Socialization, Training, Activity, and Responsibility. Go to www.akc.org/starpuppy.

The **AKC Therapy Dog** program recognizes all American Kennel Club dogs and their owners who have given their time and helped people by volunteering as a therapy dog-and-owner team. The AKC Therapy Dog program is an official American Kennel Club title awarded to dogs that have worked to improve the lives of the people they have visited. The AKC Therapy Dog title (AKC ThD) can be earned by dogs that have been certified by recognized therapy dog organizations. For more information, visit www.akc.org/akctherapydog.

Index

AMERICAN KENNEL CLUB®

Advocating for the purebred dog as a family companion, advancing canine health and well-being, working to protect the rights of all dog owners and promoting responsible dog ownership, the **American Kennel Club:**

Sponsors more than **22,000 sanctioned events** annually including conformation, agility, obedience, rally, tracking, lure coursing, earthdog, herding, field trial, hunt test, and coonhound events

Features a **10-step Canine Good Citizen® program** that rewards dogs who have good manners at home and in the community

Has reunited more than **400,000** lost pets with their owners through the AKC Companion Animal Recovery - visit **www.akccar.org**

Created and supports the AKC Canine Health Foundation, which funds research projects using the more than **$22 million** the AKC has donated since 1995 - visit **www.akcchf.org**

Joins **animal lovers** through education, outreach and grant-making via the AKC Humane Fund - visit **www.akchumanefund.org**

We're more than champion dogs. We're the dog's champion.

www.akc.org